The Music Master

Ensemble Book

By

Graham Bennett
Author, Composer & Publisher

This Book is dedicated to my dear friend
Mrs Margaret Hadfield

The Music Master
Ensemble Book

First Published 2006
by Egon Publishers

First Published 2008
by The Music Master Publications

ISBN: 978-0-9559184-7-6

Printed for the publisher by
Howard Digital Limited
Business Centre West, Unit 5a, Avenue One, Herts. SG6 2HB

Contents

Chapter One

...Welcome to the Composer's Toolbox...

This chapter provides detailed explanations, tasks and tools on:

- Understanding key signatures
- Intervals in music
- Triads, chord inversions
- Chromatic harmonies, dominant 7ths, diminished 7ths, major and minor
- The French, German, Italian augmented 6th chords
- The Neapolitan 6th

At the end of the chapter you will find 'The Cosmopolitan Crossword' which will test your knowledge of harmony.

Working out Major and Minor key Signatures

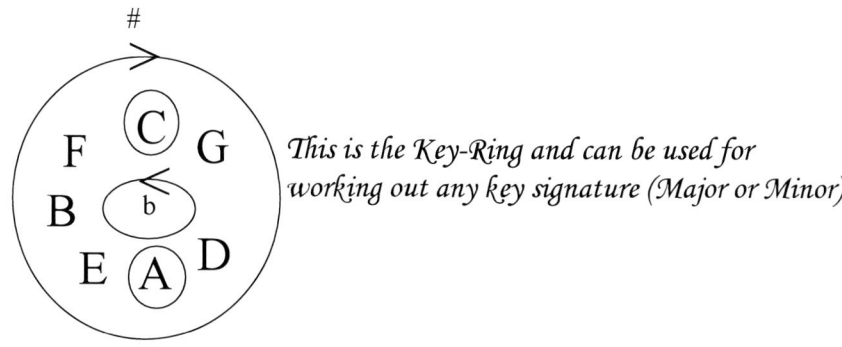

This is the Key-Ring and can be used for working out any key signature (Major or Minor)

For Major keys, put your finger on C and count round the circle (clockwise for # and anti clockwise for ♭)
For Minor keys, put your finger on A and count round the circle (clockwise for # and anti clockwise for ♭)

Example 1: How many sharps does B Major have ?.... begin on C and count round clockwise to B.
The answer is 5 sharps.

Example 2: How many flats does F Minor have?....begin on A and count round anti clockwise to F.
The answer is 4 flats.

Now that you can work out how many # or ♭ are present in any major or minor key, you
can remember the order for writing them by using the rhyme below....

> # Father Christmas Gave Dad An Electric Blanket
>
> ♭ Blanket Exploded And Dad Got Cold Feet

If we know that F Minor has 4 flats we can look at the rhyme above to work out that the 4
flats = B,E,A,D (Blanket, Exploded, And, Dad)

Similarly, if we know that B Major has 5 sharps we can look at the rhyme above to work
out that the 5 sharps = F,C,G,D,A (Father, Christmas, Gave Dad, An)

Where to write the # and ♭ on the stave.

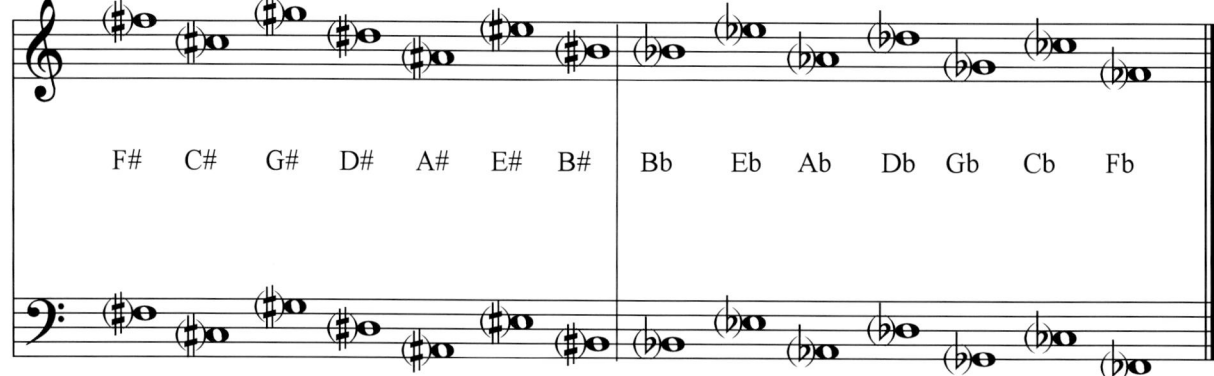

Naming and writing Key signatures

The Major Key with four
sharps = _____

Re-write this key signature
correctly in the Bass Clef

The Minor Key with three
flats = _____

Re-write this key signature correctly
in the Treble Clef

The Major Key with five
sharps = _____

Re-write this key signature
correctly in the Bass Clef

The Major Key with two
flats = _____

Re-write this Key signature
correctly in the Treble Clef

The Major Key with four
flats = _____

Re-write this Key signature
correctly in the Bass Clef

The Minor Key with three
sharps = _____

Re-write this Key signature
correctly in the Treble Clef

Intervals...

An Interval is the Distance between two notes in music.

It is important to understand intervals for a variety of reasons......
a) Intervals provide melodic shape which helps the performer to sight read confidently.
b) To develop a feeling for the melodic phrase and dynamics, rising intervals often create a feeling of crescendo and falling intervals a diminuendo. Often you can locate the start and finish of a phrase from the use of intervallic movement. (ie: where is the highest note, where is the lowest note)

This is an interval. (the distance between the notes F and C = 5th)

When calculating an interval always start from the bottom (or lowest) note and count upwards. (for example: F, G, A, B, C = 5th)

This is an example of how intervals can create a feeling of dynamic and melodic shape. Below we can see a variety of 3rds and 4ths which help the melody rise and fall. The dynamics are created from the melodic shape (mf at the top, p at the bottom) and the phrasing represents the two shapes created by the melody.

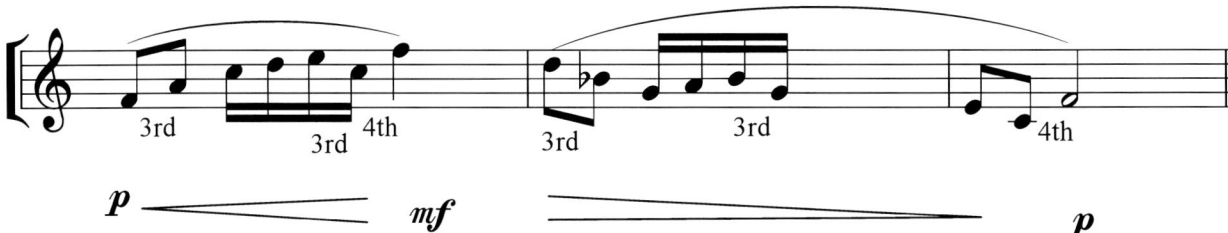

Look at the melody below and see if you can answer Questions a)-d)

a) How many 6ths can you find? _____

b) How many 4ths can you find? _____

c) How many 2nds can you find? _____

d) What is the largest interval? _____

4

To calculate whether an interval is Major or Minor
just follow the steps below...

> *1) Work out the distance between the notes. ie: is the interval a 2nd, 3rd, etc...*
>
> *2) Look at the LOWEST note of the interval. This note is called the KEY-NOTE.*
>
> *3) Use the Key-note and think MAJOR key signature and MINOR key signature. (for example: the key note is F so I work out the key signature of F Major and F Minor.)*
>
> *4) Look at the top note of the interval. Does the top note have a sharp or flat which would make it fit the Major Key or the Minor Key? This determines whether the interval is Major or Minor.*

Here is an explained example:

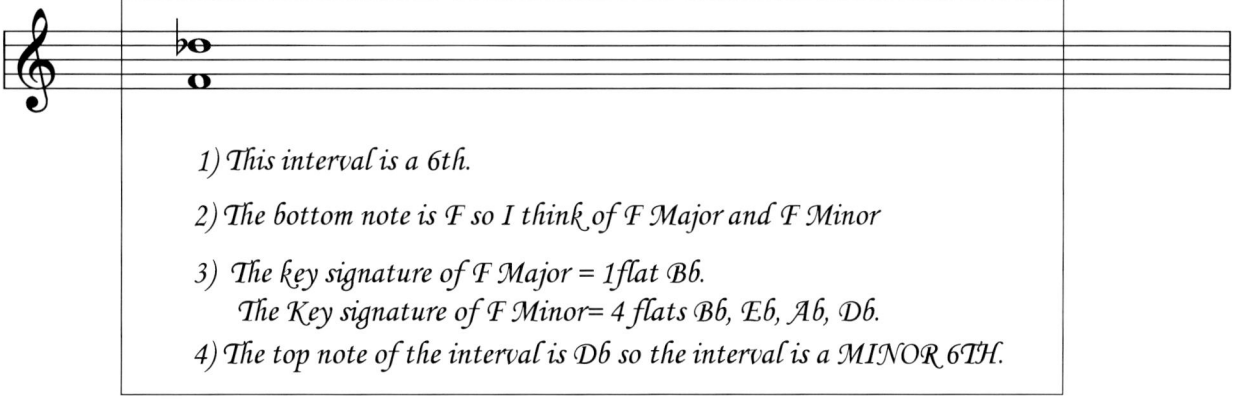

> *1) This interval is a 6th.*
>
> *2) The bottom note is F so I think of F Major and F Minor*
>
> *3) The key signature of F Major = 1 flat Bb.*
> *The Key signature of F Minor= 4 flats Bb, Eb, Ab, Db.*
> *4) The top note of the interval is Db so the interval is a MINOR 6TH.*

The following intervals can be major, minor, augmented, diminished: (2nd, 3rd, 6th, 7th) The intervals 4th, 5th and 8th are never major or minor, they are known as Perfect because the top note of the interval is present in both the major and minor keys. Intervals bigger than a major or perfect, can become Augmented and intervals smaller than a minor or perfect can become Diminished. (see examples below)

This is a perfect 5th   *This is a perfect 4th*   *This is a diminished 3rd*

This is an augmented 2nd   *This is a augmented 5th*   *This is a diminshed 8th*

Understanding Triads and their Inversions

A Triad is a chord build of three notes. (1st, 3rd and 5th notes of the scale)

The triads below represent the (root position triads) in C major. They are also known as 5/3 chords because of the intervals between the bottom and top notes, and bottom and middle notes.

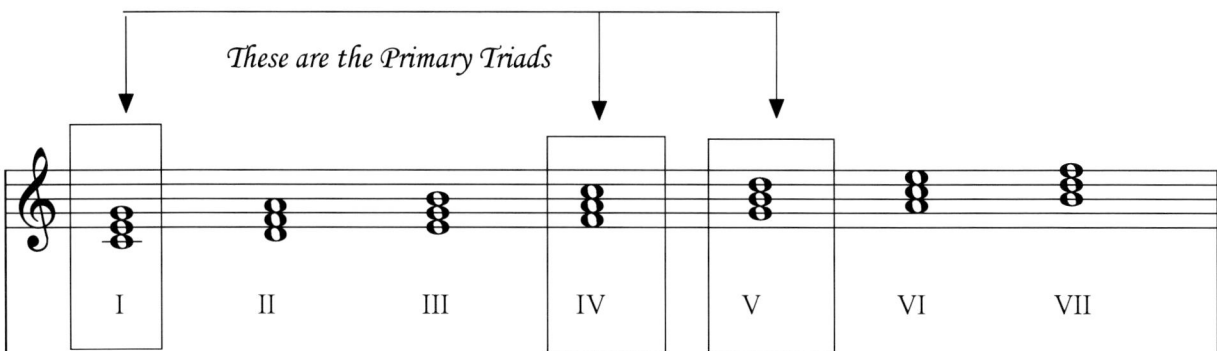

These are the Primary Triads

I   II   III   IV   V   VI   VII

The triads below represent the (1st inversion triads) in C major. They are also known as 6/3 chords because of the intervals between the bottom and top notes, and bottom and middle notes. 1st inversion triads are created by turning the triad upside down so that the 3rd note is at the bottom.

I   II   III   IV   V   VI   VII

The triads below represent the (2nd inversion triads) in C major. They are also known as 6/4 chords because of the intervals between the bottom and top notes, and bottom and middle notes. 2nd inversion triads are created by turning the triad upside down again so that the 5th note is at the bottom.

I   II   III   IV   V   VI   VII

Creating Dominant 7th and Diminished 7th chords

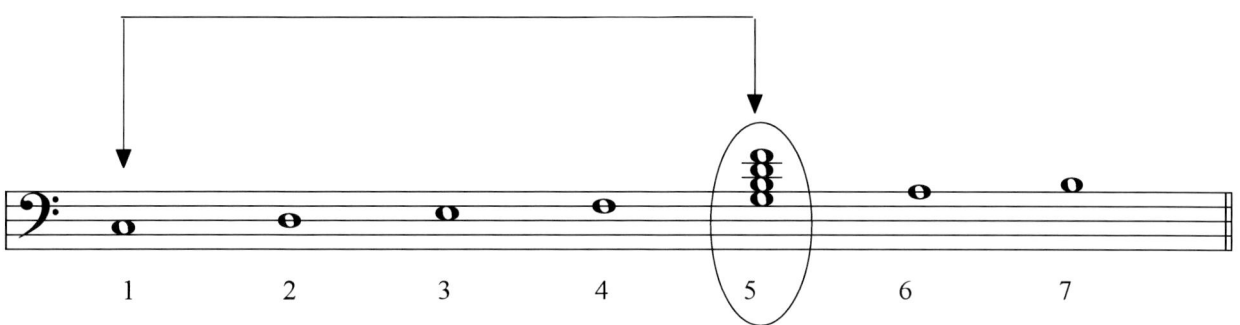

1   2   3   4   5   6   7

This chord represents the dominant 7th chord in the key of C Major. It is a triad built on the 5th note of the scale with an added 7th.

When creating a triad you always count up from the bass note. As G is the bass note, the notes in the chord = G (1st) B (3rd) D (5th) and F (7th)

C Major has no sharps or flats in the key signature so it is not necessary to add any accidentals.

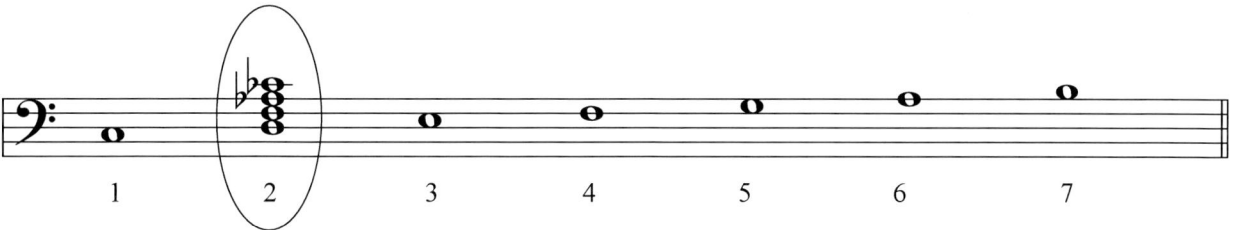

1   2   3   4   5   6   7

This chord represents a diminished 7th chord built from the 2nd note of the scale in C Major.

Diminished 7th chords can be created on any note of the scale, it is a triad with an added 7th but the intervals between each note create a minor 3rd interval. If we look at the notes present in the chord above (counting from the bass note up) we have D-F (a minor 3rd interval) F-Ab (a minor 3rd interval) Ab -Cb (a minor 3rd interval)

Triads....Major, Minor, Augmented, Diminished

The patterns below are the same for ALL Major and Minor Scales.

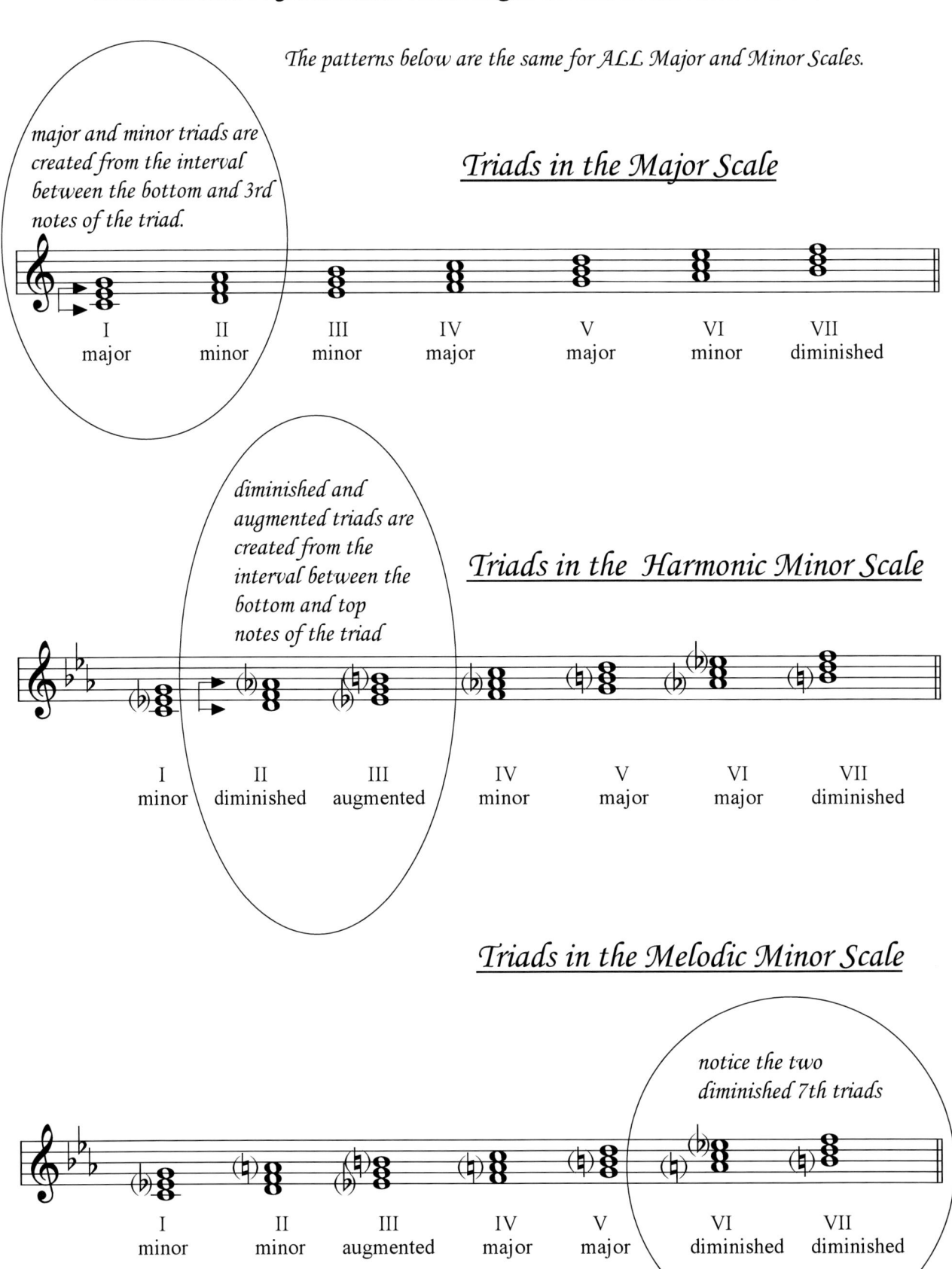

major and minor triads are created from the interval between the bottom and 3rd notes of the triad.

Triads in the Major Scale

I	II	III	IV	V	VI	VII
major	minor	minor	major	major	minor	diminished

diminished and augmented triads are created from the interval between the bottom and top notes of the triad

Triads in the Harmonic Minor Scale

I	II	III	IV	V	VI	VII
minor	diminished	augmented	minor	major	major	diminished

Triads in the Melodic Minor Scale

notice the two diminished 7th triads

I	II	III	IV	V	VI	VII
minor	minor	augmented	major	major	diminished	diminished

Understanding Chromatic Harmonies.....

The Augmented 6th chords....German, French, Italian

German	Italian	French
C Major	C Major	C Major

This is the German Augmented 6th chord in C Major. (the root of the chord is a minor 6th above the key note,(C-Ab) there is an augmented 6th interval between the root and the top note, (Ab-F#) and **all the notes of the triad are present. (Ab, C, Eb)**

This is the Italian Augmented 6th chord in C Major. (the root of the chord is a minor 6th above the key note, (C-Ab) there is an augmented 6th interval between the root and the top note, (Ab-F#) but the **5th note of the triad (the Eb) is missing.**

This is the French Augmented 6th chord in C Major. (the root of the chord is a minor 6th above the key note, (C-Ab) there is an augmented 6th interval between the root and the top note, (Ab-F#) but the **5th note has been lowered a semitone. (Eb becomes D)**

The Neapolitan 6th chord

Diatonic chords with an added 7th

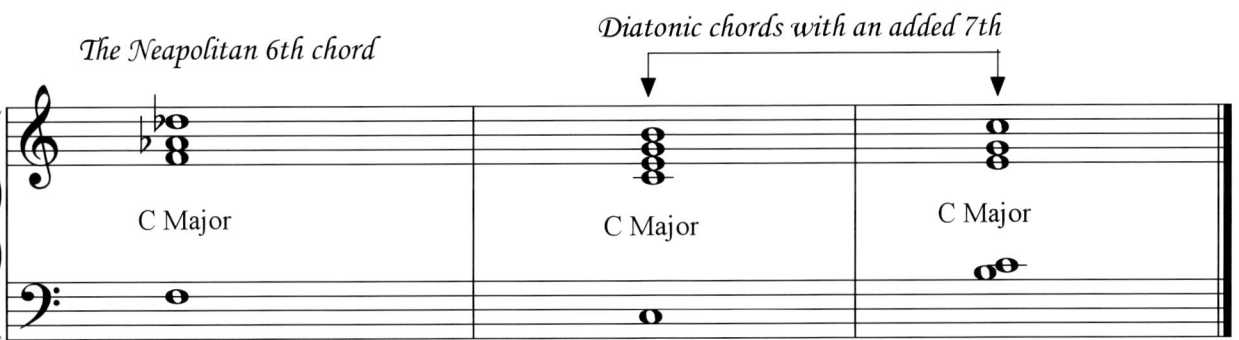

C Major	C Major	C Major

This is the Neapolitan 6th in C Major. (this chord is a **major triad based on the flattened supertonic (chord II) of the key in 1st inversion)**

This is a 7th chord in C Major and is built from **four notes** (the notes of a standard triad with an added 7th)

As chords with an added 7th consist of four notes, you can turn the chord upside down 3 times to create 1st, 2nd and 3rd inversion. The example above is in 3rd inversion.

Welcome to
'The Cosmopolitan Crossword'

This puzzle is based around the Augmented 6th chords also known as the Italian, French and German, though you will also find examples of the Neapolitan 6th.

To complete this puzzle first you need to name the different chords on the next page. Once you have done this you can check your answers by trying to fit them into the crossword on the last page. If you are correct with your answers you will be able to complete the crossword using the clues provided at the end of the puzzle.

Have fun !!!!!!

Crazy about chords....

First you need to work out which chord is present in each bar by writing either French, Italian, German or Neapolitan, and then use the clues to fit your answers into the crossword on the next page. (notice that (3 down) is a different type of chord and requires a different answer. Have fun and Good Luck !!!

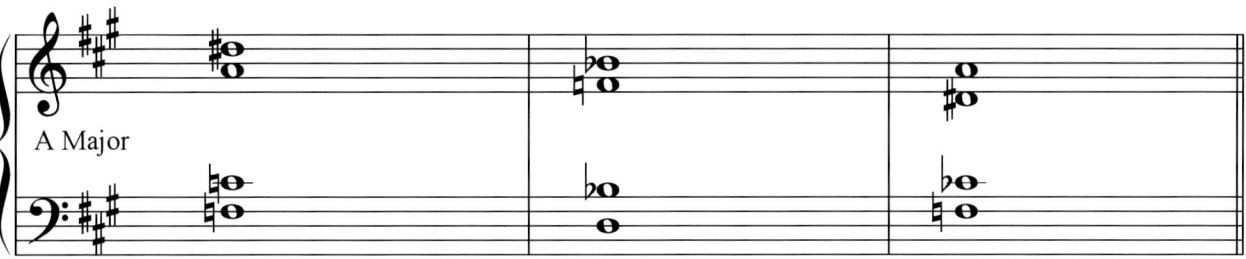

1 across = _____   2 down = _____   4 across = _____

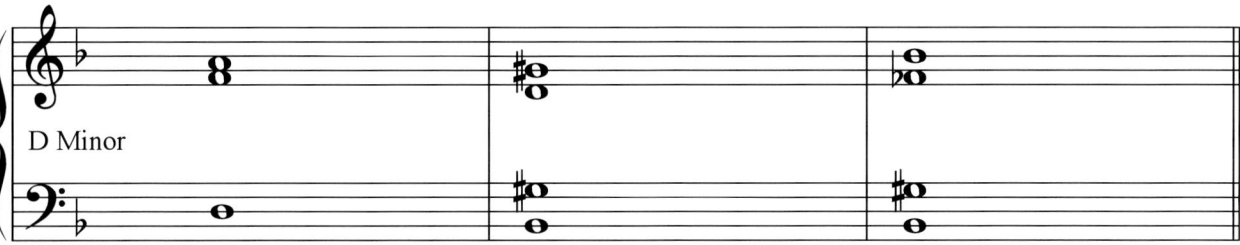

3 down = The Tonic _____   5 down = _____   6 across = _____

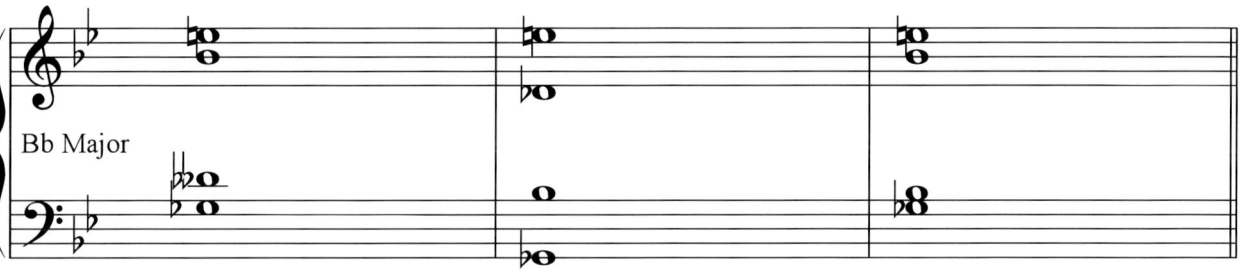

7 across = _____   8 down = _____   9 down = _____

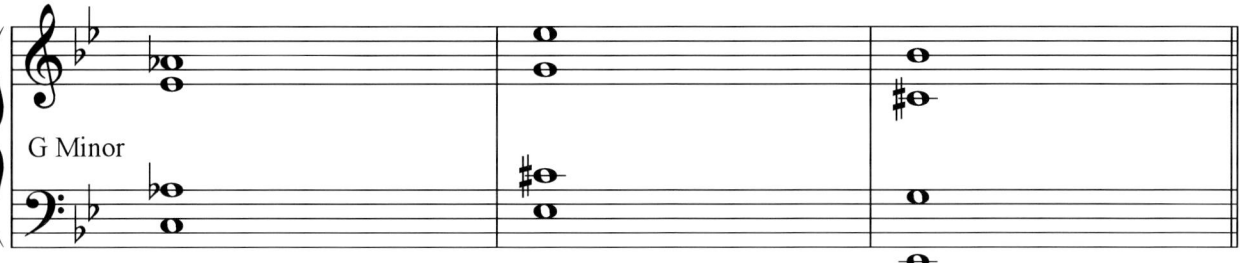

10 = down _____   11 across = _____   12 across = _____

The Cosmopolitan Composer's Crossword

To complete this puzzle you need to fit your answers from the previous page into the crossword below and then use the clues at the bottom to find the missing answers.

13 down = _____ are clusters of notes played simultaneously (6)

14 down = This Augmented _____ is present in the French, Italian and German (5)

15 down = _____ is the relationship between different notes played together (7)

16 across = Two notes of the same pitch joined together is called a _____(3)

17 across = _____ are different musical signs which represent a silence in music (5)

Chapter Two

...Composing for the Electronic Keyboard...

This chapter will teach you how to write a complete piece for electronic keyboard:

- *An understanding of the electronic keyboard.*
- *Manipulating sampled sounds, rhythmic effects, and chord accompaniments*
- *Learning about blues notes and the blues harmonies*
- *How to notate a piece for electronic keyboard*

At the end of the chapter 'The Composer's word search' will help you learn the key words and tools most commonly used when composing a piece.

Writing for the Electronic Keyboard...

Writing music for the electronic keyboard is very different from writing for the pianoforte. Often there is only one line of conventional notation, but there are many signs and symbols which tell the performer how the piece should be played. The electronic keyboard is a sampler, the sound effects, rhythms and accompaniments have been pre-recorded and programmed into the keyboard data base, the performer is required to understand the signs and symbols and the performance is created from manipulating those sounds.

Below is an example of a melody written for electronic keyboard. The VOICE refers to the instrumental sound to be used when playing this melody, the STYLE refers to the rhythmic beat and background accompaniment, the letters underneath the melody refer to the chord changes (major and minor), the DRUM FILL IN, this tool is present on most keyboards and creates a rhythmic improvisation based on the Style beat, and the FADE OUT is controlled by turning the volume wheel to reduce the sound level.

Voice = Alto Sax

Style = 8bt modern

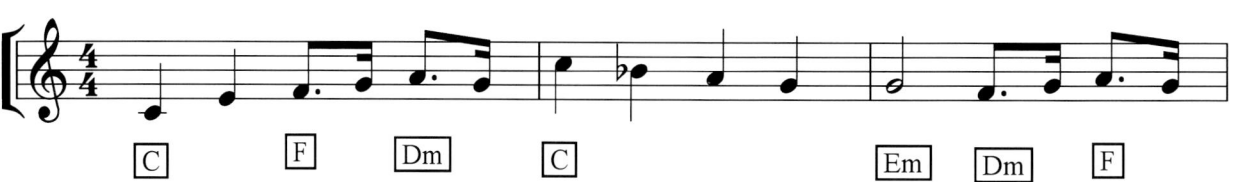

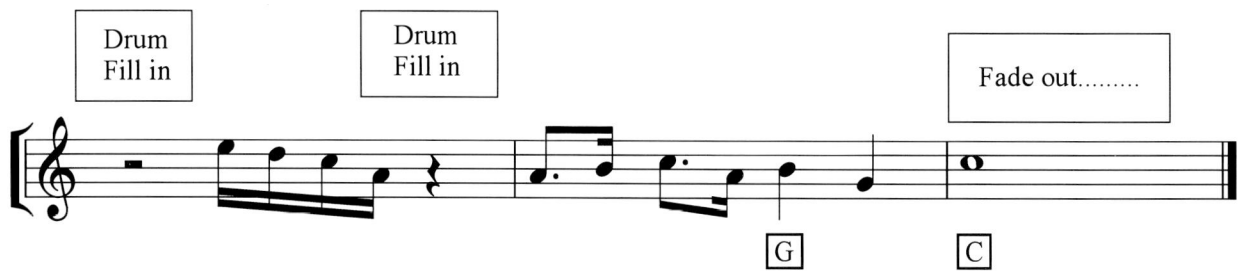

When you are writing for the electronic keyboard, it is possible to change the STYLE beat and VOICE commands during performance, this is a very good way of creating contrasting sections within a piece. It is also possible to create chord changes during long rests within the bar to provide additional interest to the texture.

14

Understanding Blues Notes and Blues Harmonies

Below is an example of a Blues Scale starting on C

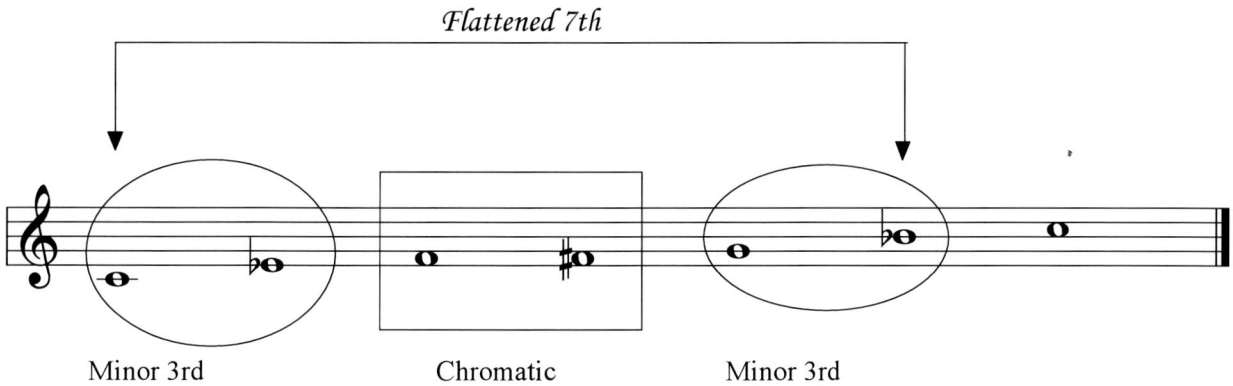

Blues tunes are normally composed over 12-bars which are harmonised using three different chords known as the PRIMARY TRIADS (I, IV and V). These triads are based on the 1st, the 4th and the 5th notes of the scale. (also known as Tonic, Subdominant and Dominant)

When you are harmonising a melody written for electronic keyboard, the chords are normally indicated using letters underneath the tune. If the letter includes an 'm' next to it this means the chord will be minor and if there is only a note name (for example C) then the chord will be major.
Below are some examples based on the scale of C Major....

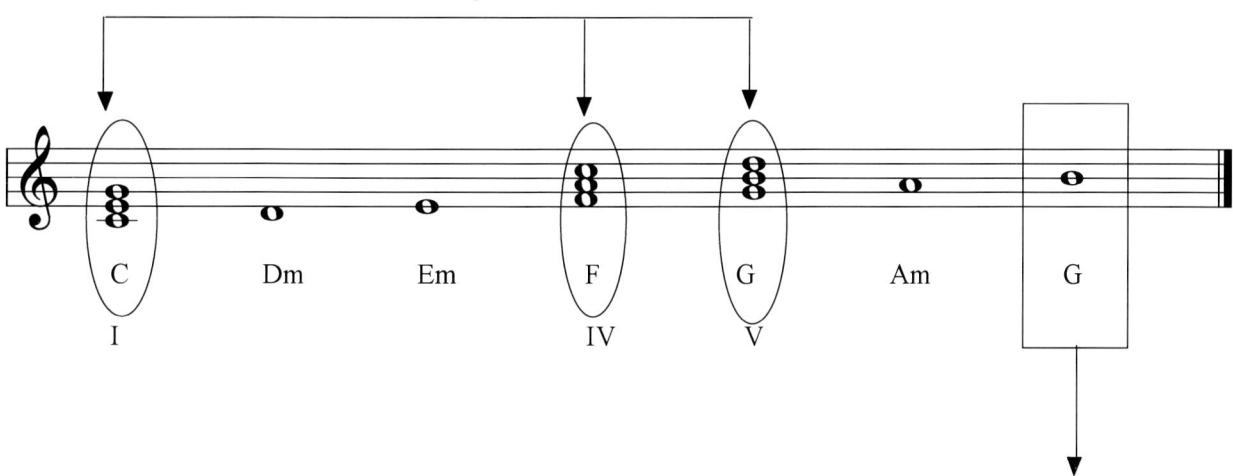

Here I chose the chord of G. The note B is present in the triad of G which is also chord V in the scale of C Major. Chord V is one of the primary triads, and it is good to finish on a strong harmony.

The 12-bar Blues

Task One: *Create a 12-bar blues melody for electronic keyboard using notes from the primary triads I, IV, and V, combined with notes from the blues scale.*

Task Two: *Choose a suitable 'blues style' rhythmic beat and harmonise your melody by adding a variety of LH chords (represent the chords using letters underneath the melody)*

Voice =

Style =

chord I   chord I   chord I

chord I   chord IV   chord IV

chord V   chord V   chord IV

chord IV   chord I   chord I

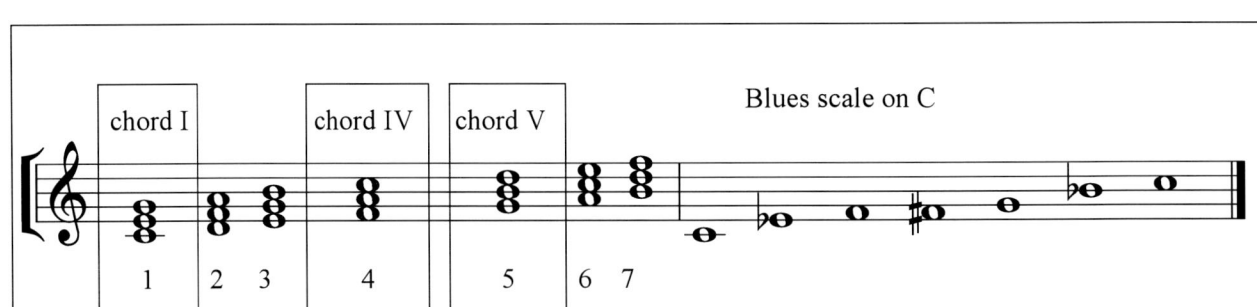

chord I   chord IV   chord V   Blues scale on C

1   2   3   4   5   6   7

16

Examples of the 12-bar Blues

Voice = Trumpet

Style = 4/4 blues

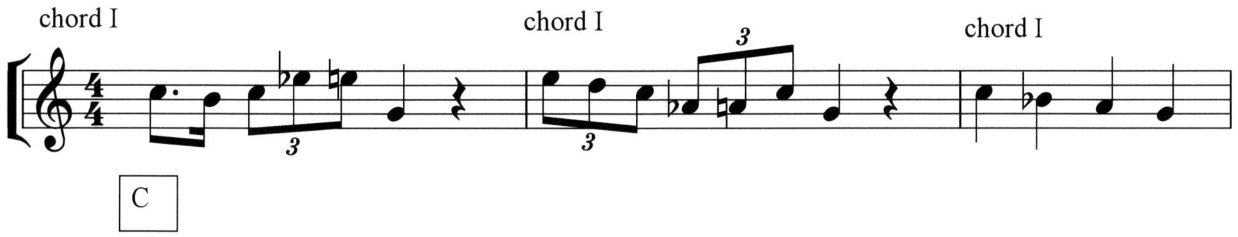

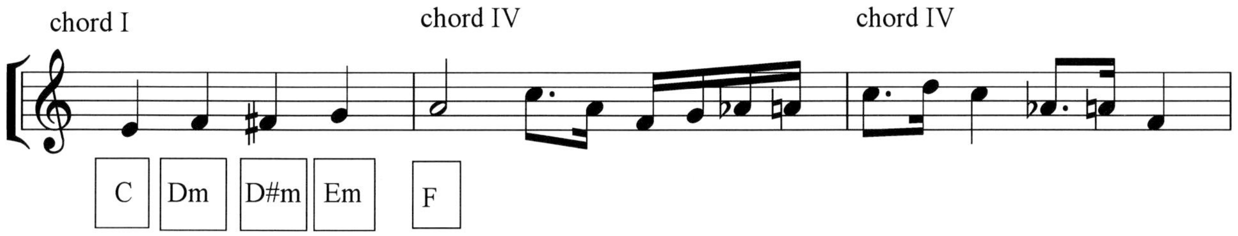

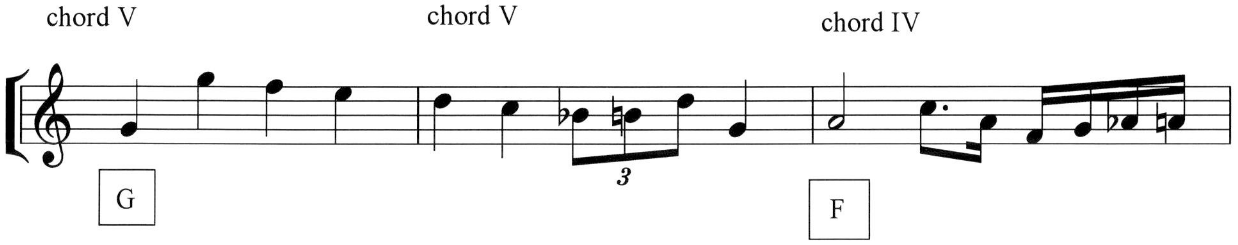

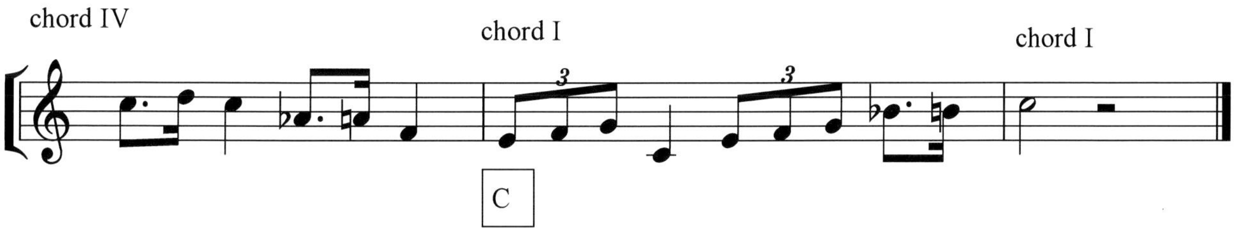

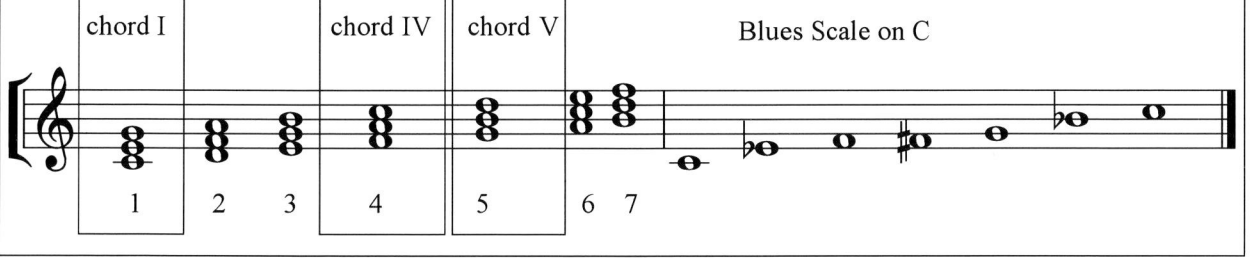

The Composer's word search

To complete this puzzle try and find all of the words below in the word search....good luck !!!

T	A	I	N	S	T	R	U	M	E	N	T	H	S	U
E	R	B	S	T	P	I	T	C	H	C	U	A	E	S
M	H	A	M	R	N	V	M	X	N	R	N	R	Q	T
P	Y	I	N	V	E	R	S	I	O	N	E	M	U	A
O	T	M	A	S	Y	S	J	Y	T	H	L	O	E	C
R	H	X	C	D	P	M	T	U	E	A	O	N	N	C
Y	M	C	O	U	R	O	L	S	T	E	T	Y	C	A
R	F	L	A	T	W	D	S	W	E	K	A	I	E	T
W	E	E	B	J	C	U	N	I	X	N	G	A	O	O
M	I	F	K	R	B	L	L	A	T	G	E	L	J	N
E	R	S	R	S	H	A	R	P	U	I	L	M	E	B
K	Y	A	G	E	J	T	R	N	R	Z	O	H	R	A
M	D	Y	N	A	M	I	C	S	E	F	L	N	M	A
V	O	P	I	G	H	O	R	F	Y	T	Q	W	I	O
B	P	U	L	S	E	N	A	T	U	R	A	L	S	E

Tempo	Staccato	Sequence
Rhythm	Imitation	Pitch
Flat	Legato	Clef
Melody	Texture	Range
Transposition	Modulation	Instrument
Sharp	Rests	Harmony
Dynamics	Inversion	Pulse
Natural	Tune	Bar

Chapter Three

...Writing for string quartet...

This chapter will teach you how to compose a complete piece for string quartet consisting of four contrasting movements. Some of the tools and techniques explored in the chapter include:

- Writing in the alto clef for the viola
- Understanding musical textures: monophonic, polyphonic, heterophonic, homophonic, and how to apply them in the composition.
- String writing techniques: arco, pizzicato, double stopping, string crossing, using harmonics, tremolandos and con sordini.
- A detailed study of musical ornamentation
- Using different types of rhythm: cross-rhythms, syncopation, rhythmic augmentation and diminution between instrumental parts.
- Modulations: how to prepare for a change of key within the movement.

At the end of the chapter 'The Symphony Sizzler' will challenge your knowledge of music theory and musical instruments.

Writing for String Quartet

A string Quartet consists of four instruments:

Violin I, Violin II, Viola, Cello

Violins I and II use the treble clef, viola uses the alto clef and the cello uses the bass clef.
When you are writing for stringed instruments it is important to remember the pitch range so that you don't write notes which are unplayable. Each stringed instrument has four strings. These strings are tuned to the following notes:

Violins I and II are tuned to G, D, A, E, Viola is tuned to C, G, D, A
Cello is also tuned to C, G, D, A (but an octave lower than the viola)

Here are the ranges for the different stringed instruments:

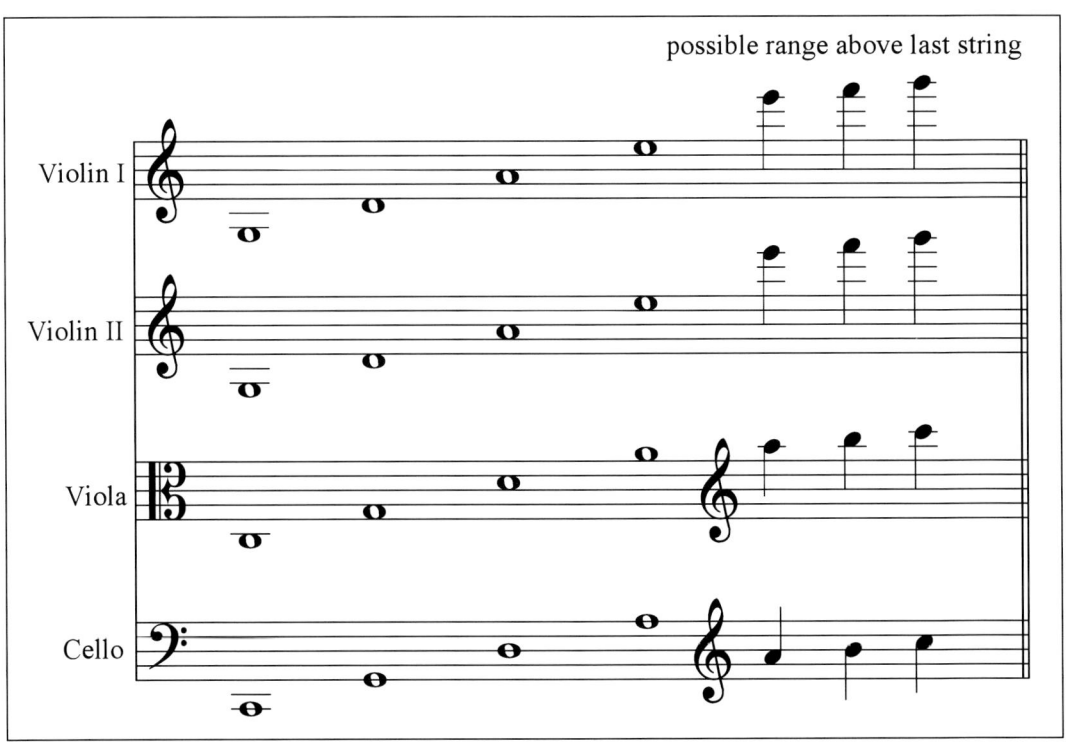

There are many different ways to write for stringed instruments, (pizzicato, arco, con sordini, double stopping, arpeggios, string crossing, harmonics....) this project will teach you how to write and explore some of these techniques.

Writing in the Alto Clef

The Alto Clef is used by the Viola.

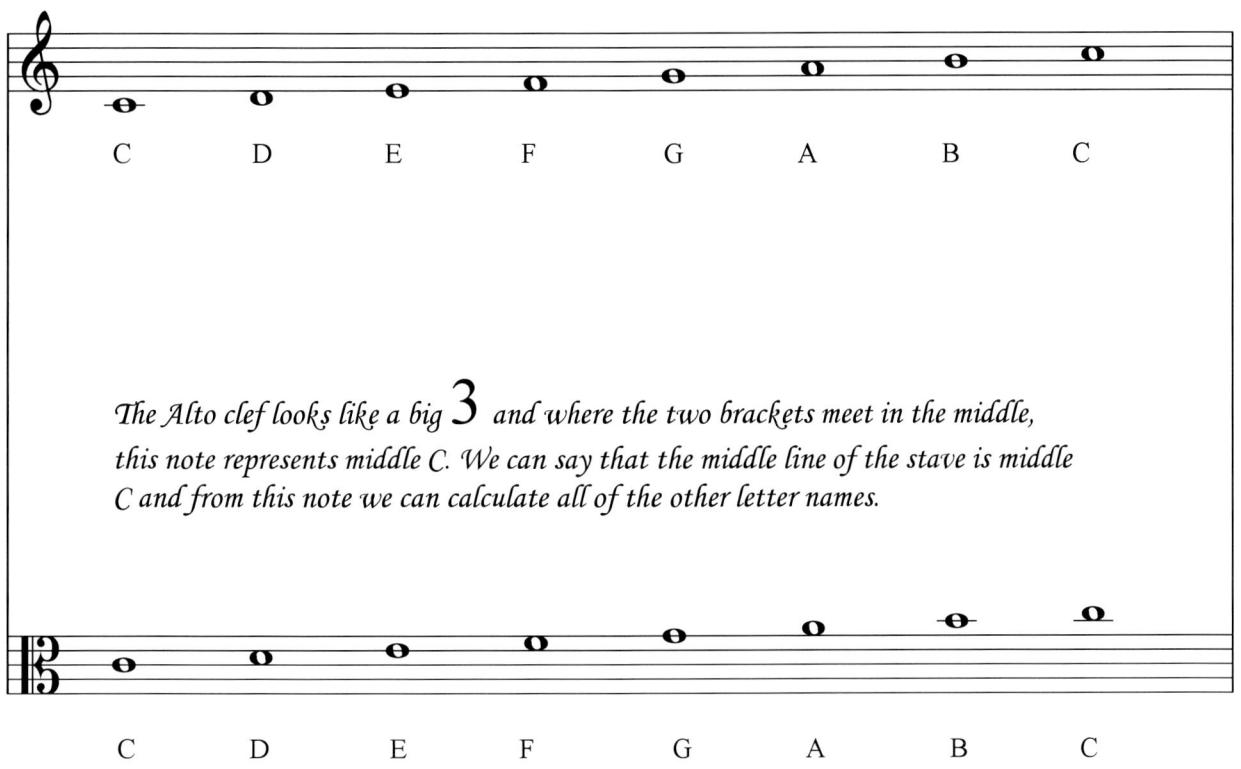

The Alto clef looks like a big **3** and where the two brackets meet in the middle, this note represents middle C. We can say that the middle line of the stave is middle C and from this note we can calculate all of the other letter names.

To help you learn the notes in the Alto Clef, try re-writing the melody below from treble clef into the alto clef. Remember to locate middle C in both clefs before you begin so that you transpose the notes into the correct octave.

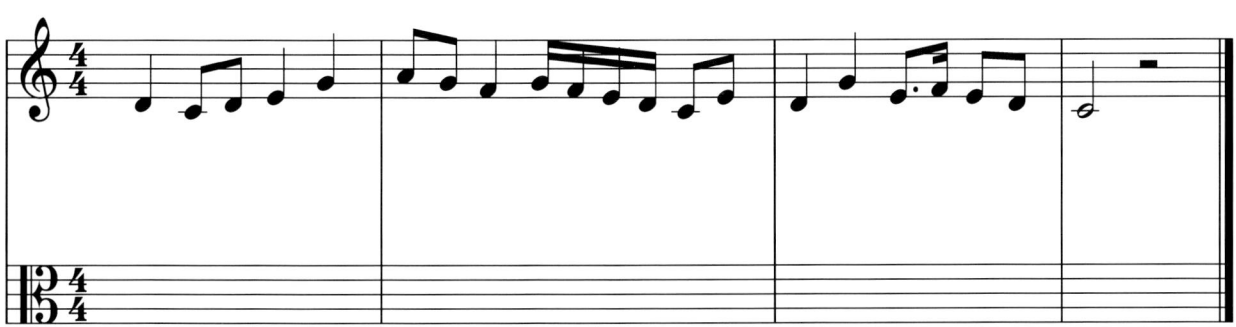

Part One: Extending motifs to create a melody

Task one   *Continue each melodic opening to create eight 4-bar tunes.*

Part Two: The Melody

Examples......

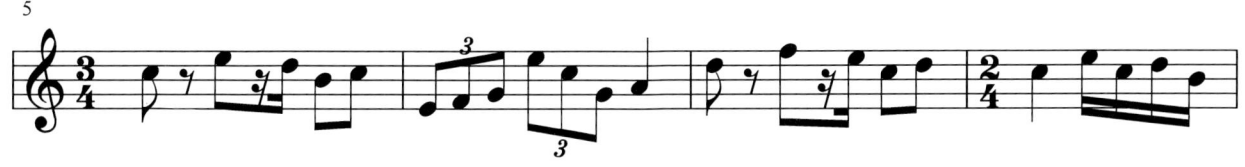

...Phonic madness...

In music there are many ways to create different musical textures. The most commonly known methods include:

Monophonic

*a single line melody played or sung by **one** musician.*

Polyphonic

***many** instruments playing different melodies at the same time.*

Heterophonic

*instruments playing the melody in the **opposite** way.*
(for example: flute plays the melody ascending, horn plays the melody descending, violins play with the bow, cellos pluck the string.)

Homophonic

*All the instruments play the **same** idea at the same time in the same way. (for example: all the strings play the same rhythm, the same melody and with the mute.)*

...1st Movement...

The 1st movement will be constructed of three main sections:

The Exposition
which 'exposes' the main melody.

The Development section
which explores texture, and a little bit of melodic variation.

The Recapitulation
which reflects the main melody and some of the features of the development section.

Task One:
Choose four contrasting bars from your main melody (try and select bars with interesting rhythmic and intervallic features). Once you have done this decide which instrument is going to begin the movement and write in your four bars using the manuscript layout provided.

Task Two:
Imitate your four bars in each instrument so that everyone has a chance to play it. This will take you up to bar 17.

Task Three:
At Bars 13 and 15 the texture should change (Heterophonic at bar 13 and then Polyphonic at bar 15) Choose which instruments you would like to use to create these textures and write in the notation.

Task Four:
The section from Bar 17-Bar 20 represents a development of your melodic ideas. Use these bars to experiment with the rhythmic and intervallic features from the four bars used at the beginning.

Task Five:
Bars 21-24 represent a homophonic texture. (you may use any part of your melody in this section, but all the instruments must play the same tune at the same time)

Task Six:
Begin by re-writing your four bars from the beginning. (you may choose to write them in a different instrument to create a contrast). Once you have done this use bars 29-32 to reflect some of the development you created in bars 17-20. In the last four bars (33-36) introduce an example of imitation between two instruments and finish with a Homophonic texture. Try and finish with chord I in the key of the movement.

Exposition of main idea

Monophonic

Development section

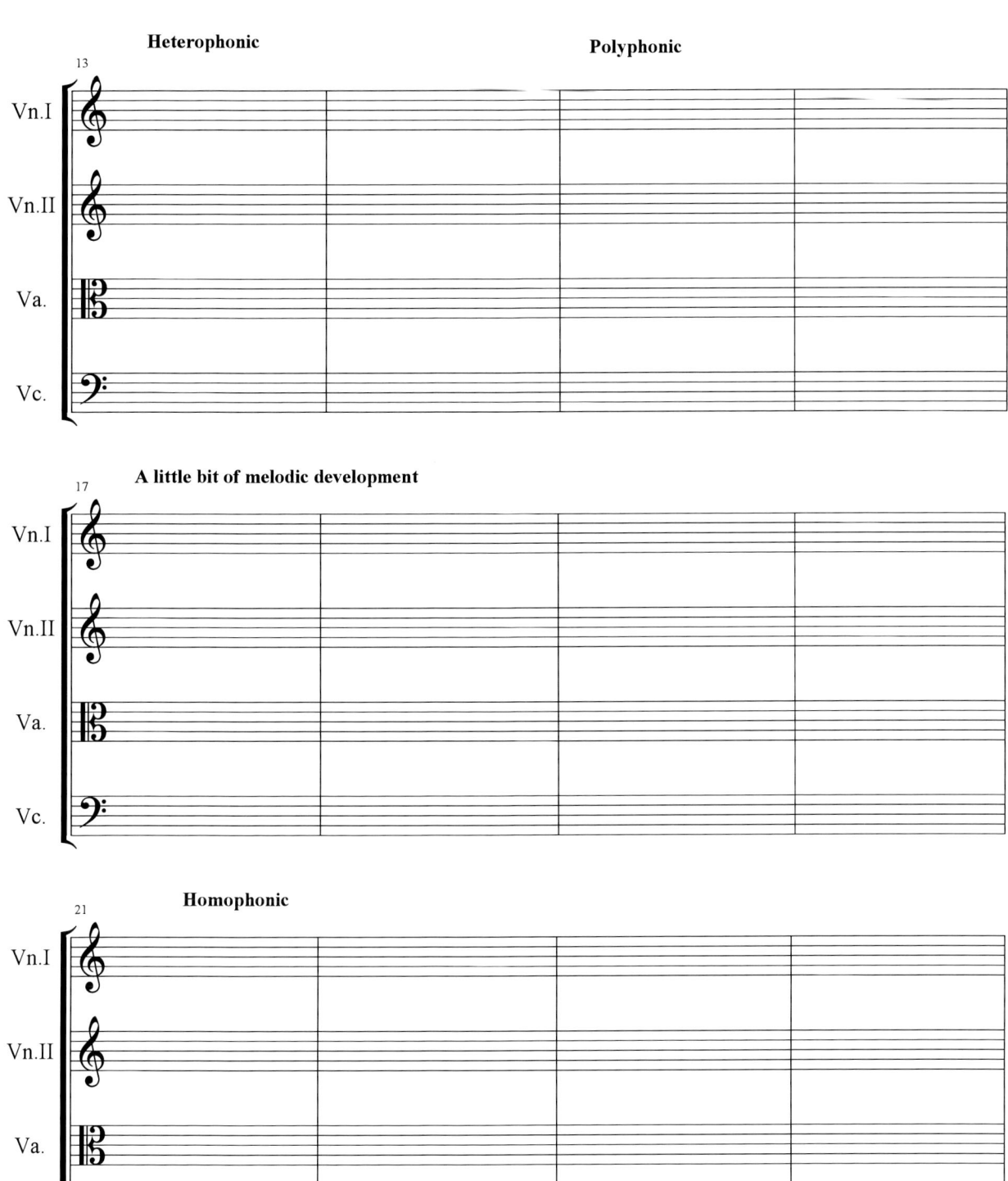

Recapitulation
(the main idea with some reference to the development section)

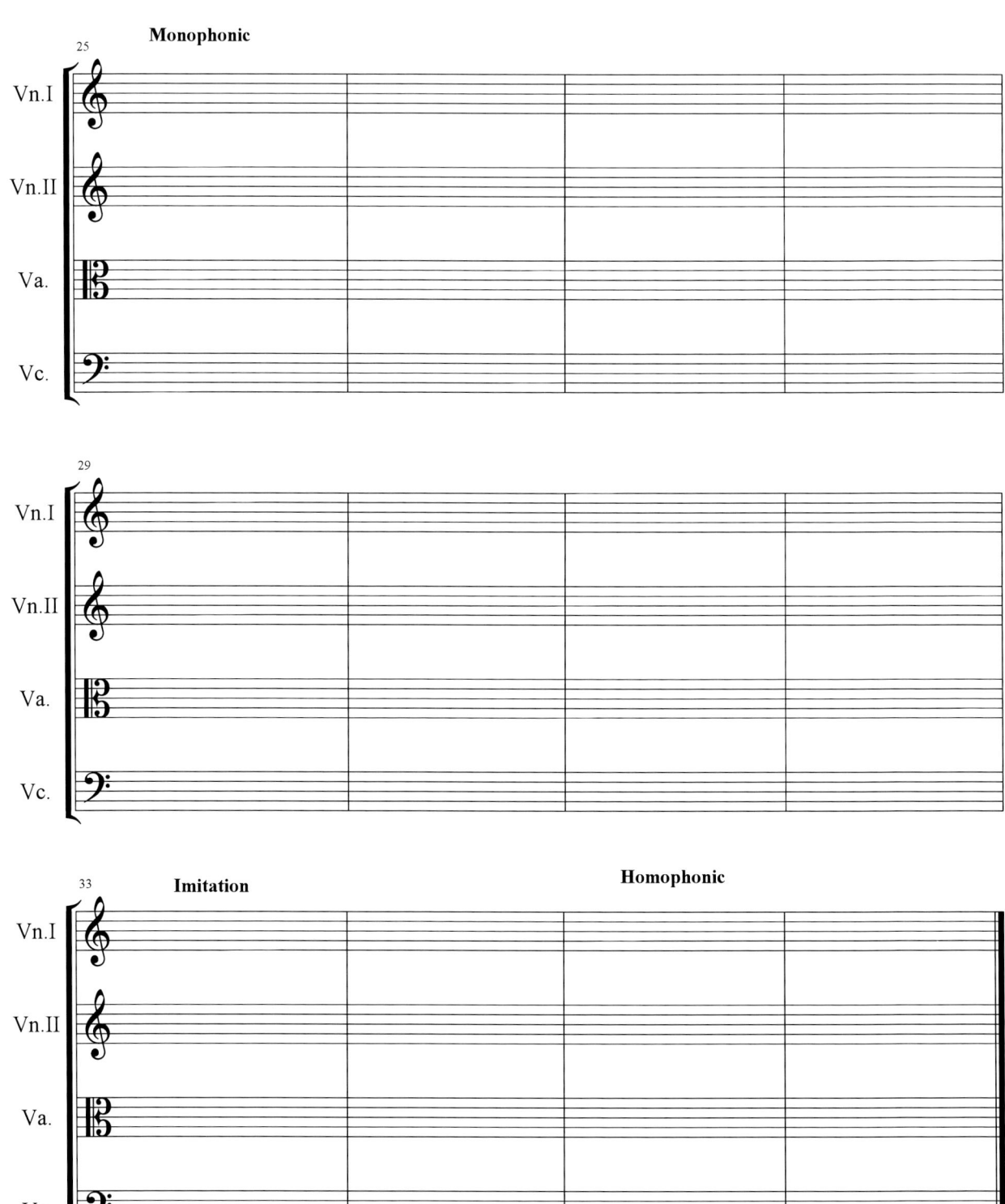

...some examples of how to create your 1st Movement...

Exposition of main idea

Development section

Recapitulation
(the main idea with some reference to the development section)

Working with rhythm

There are many ways to develop an interesting rhythmic pattern and pulse...dotted rhythms, syncopations, cross-rhythms, rhythmic augmentation and rhythmic diminution are some examples....

Syncopation is a rhythmic idea which accents the weak beat of a regular pulse (for example: the quaver between beats 2 and 3 in 4/4 time). This type of rhythm is very common in jazz, but it can be used effectively in any type of composition to create anxiety and tension between instrumental parts or to provide momentum in the melody. **Cross-rhythms** are very effective for building up tension and momentum within large textures. They represent rhythmic patterns which contrast and react against each other, thus pushing the music forward. Many composers combine cross-rhythms with melodic sequence, often mixing syncopation with irregular rhythms/changing time meters. **Rhythmic augmentation** is a way of stretching the rhythmic pattern, often through doubling the note values or tying notes across the bar. **Rhythmic diminution** is the exact opposite, condensing the rhythmic pattern through halving the note values. Often it is good to use one or the other, but if you experiment by combining both within the same texture (for example: rhythmic augmentation in the cello part and rhythmic diminution in violins I and II) you can create a lot of excitement and variety in the music.

Every type of rhythm is linked to momentum and pulse, if we understand how to manipulate the rhythmic patterns within the musical idea, then we can bring the composition to life.

Moving into different keys

Modulation is the correct term for musical ideas which pass through different keys. If the music suddenly changes key without prior preparation the audience is startled and the music doesn't flow. To avoid this, the transition into the new key needs to be anticipated a few bars before it happens. Most composers link the two keys by slowly introducing accidentals required by the new key, thus providing time for the ear to adjust without effecting the momentum of the music. The tension can be created by the amount of preparation time prior to the modulation. (for example: if there is a long, slow build up of additional accidentals over ten bars, the tension will be weaker than if the modulation occurs over two bars.)

...2nd Movement ...

To create your 2nd Movement why not begin in the Minor Key to create a nice contrast. Use this movement as an opportunity to explore different types of rhythm within the instrumental parts, develop a deeper understanding of texture and experiment with modulation.

Task One:

Choose four different bars from your main melody. Once you have done this decide which key you would like write in (choose a minor key, it can be the relative minor or another) and then write in the appropriate key signature on each stave.

Task Two:

Decide which instrument or instruments are going to begin the movement and start sketching in the notation from your chosen four bars. (As you write this movement try extending or developing your four bars)

Task Three:

Follow the manuscript layout and terminology provided to create your 2nd movement. Use the example sheets to help.

2nd Movement

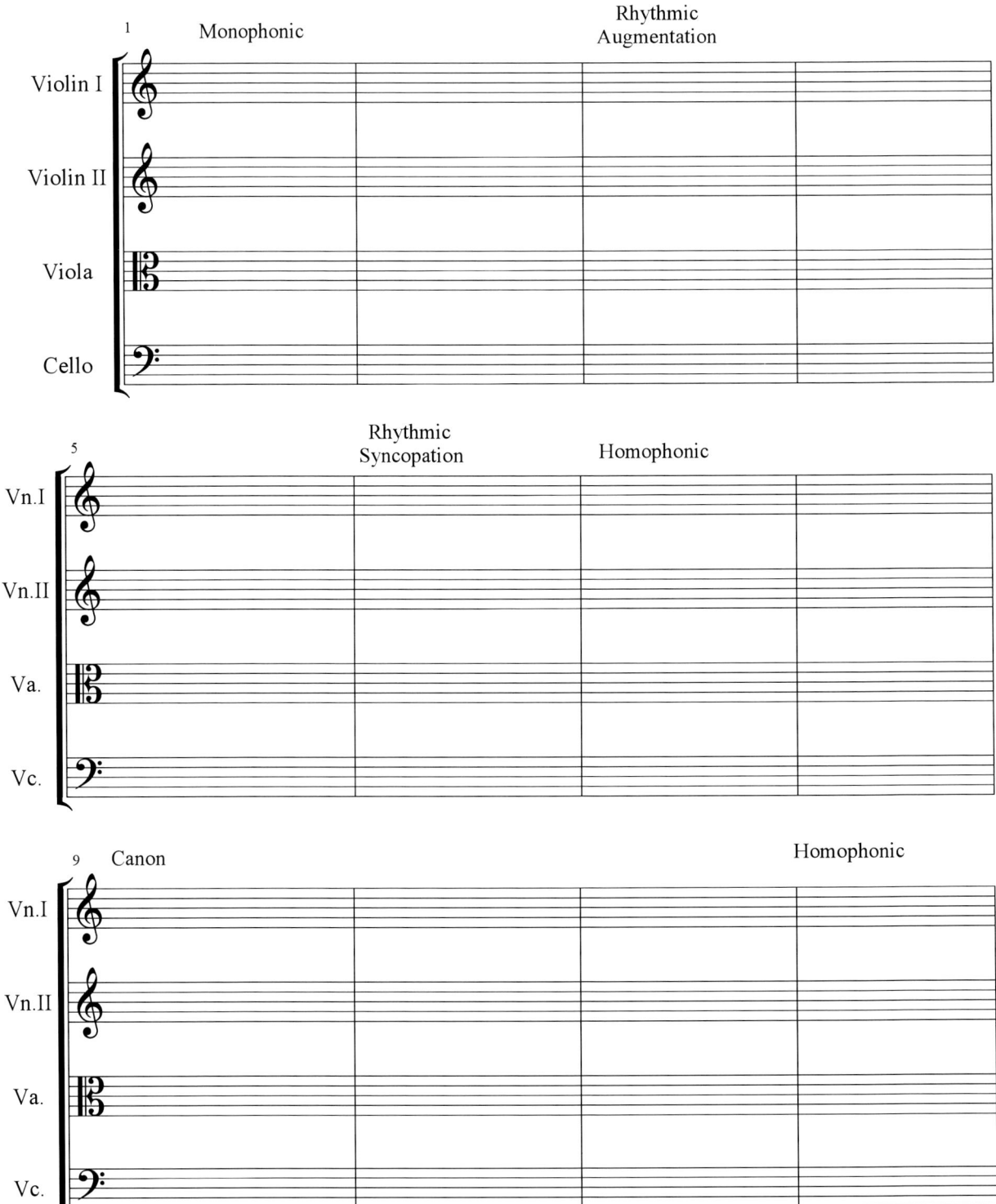

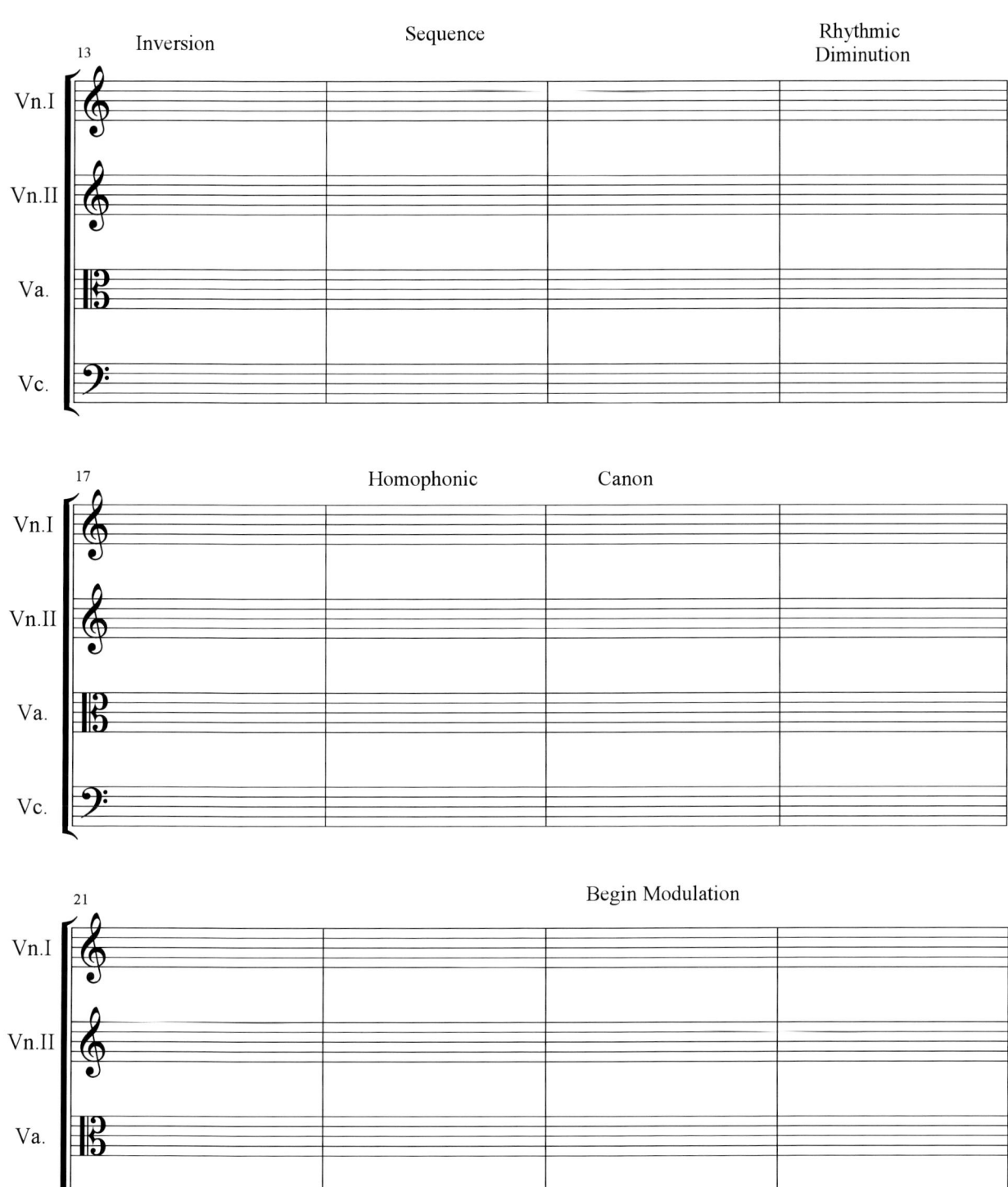

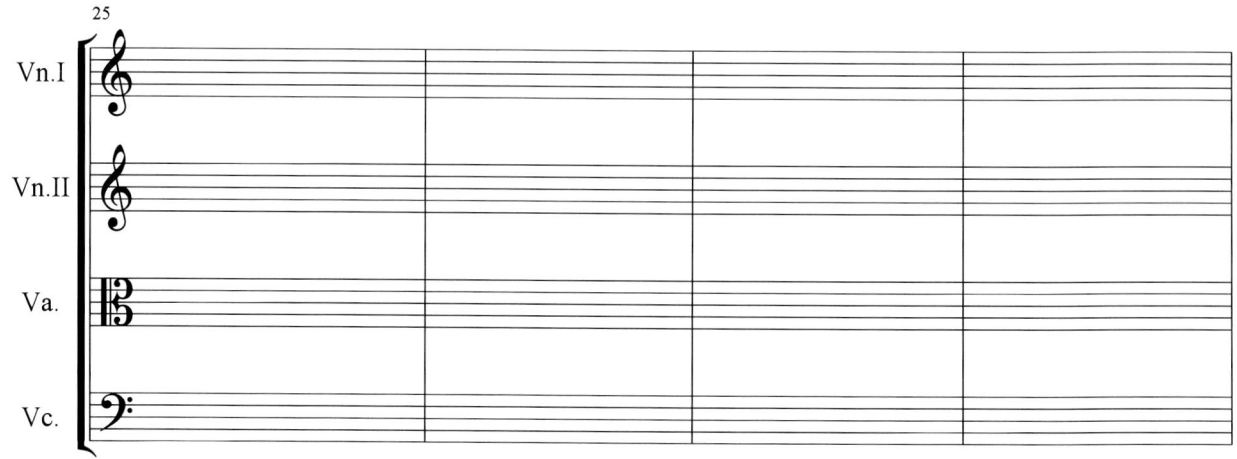

Begin a modulation back
to the Home Key   Experiment with Cross-Rhythms

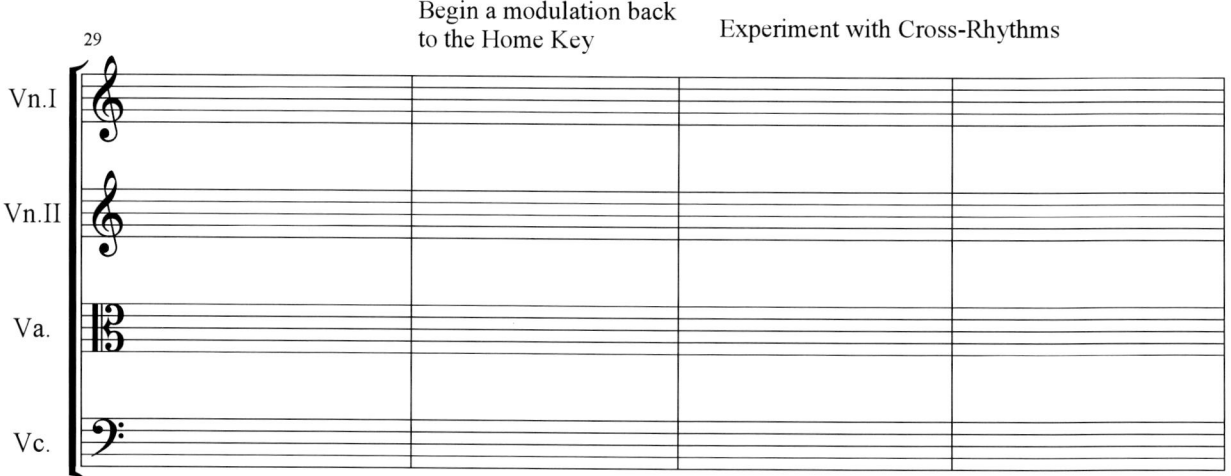

Homophonic and Sequence combined

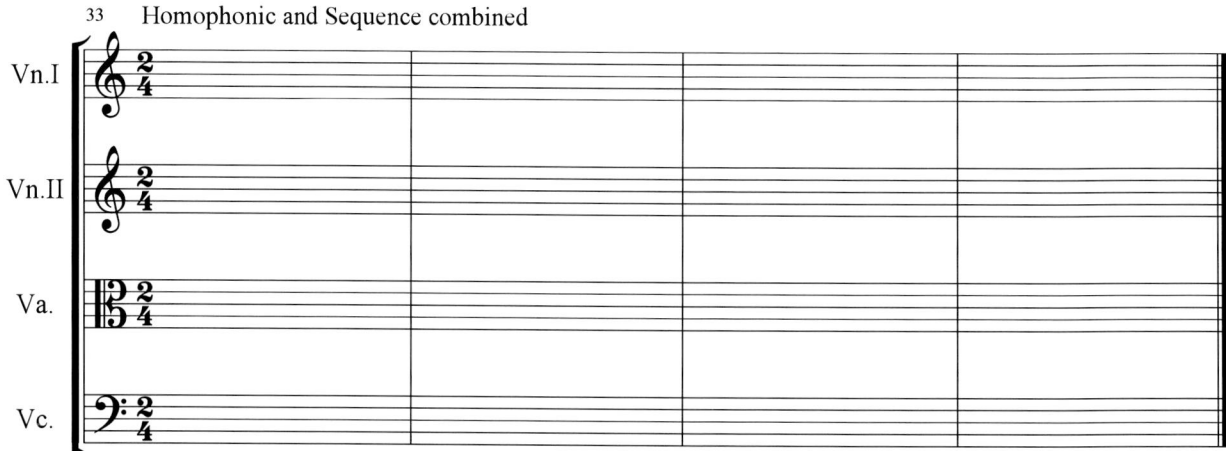

...some examples of how to create your 2nd movement...

(notice the F# and A naturals creating a modulation into G Minor)

Begin a modulation back
to the Home Key

Experiment with Cross-Rhythms

Homophonic and Sequence combined

41

Musical Ornaments

An Introduction to ornaments in music. There are 5 different ornaments most commonly used, a knowledge of their symbol and structure are essential for both performer and composer. The signs for each ornament are shown below.

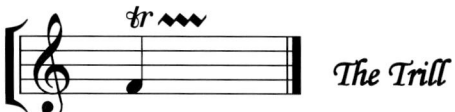 The Trill

 The Turn

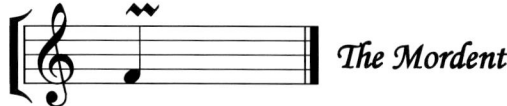 The Mordent

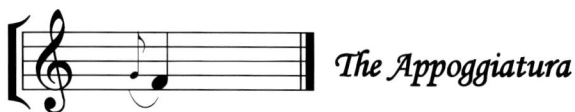 The Appoggiatura

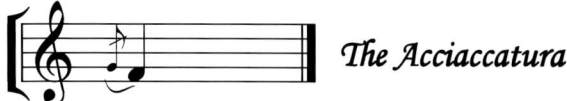 The Acciaccatura

Identifying musical ornaments
when they are written out in the music.

The Trill

This is often called a shake and is a rapid alternation of the written note a) and the note above b).

The Turn

The Turn is built from 4 notes: The note above a)
The note itself b)
The note below c)
The note itself d)

The Mordent

The Mordent is built from 3 notes: The note itself a)
The note above b)
The note itself a)

The Appoggiatura

The Appoggiatura is often referred to as a 'Passing Note'.
It takes half the value of the note it proceeds and creates a smoother melodic line. a) and b)

The Acciaccatura

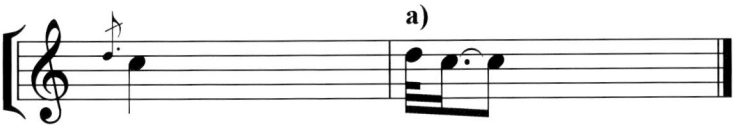

The Acciaccatura is often referred to as a 'Grace Note'.
This ornament is played very quick, normally in the value of a demisemiquaver. a)

The Trill and the Turn in more detail....

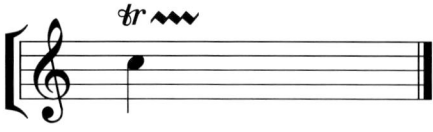

As we already know 'The Trill' is often called a shake, a word which describes the way it should be played....to shake or to alternate rapidly between two adjacent notes.

There are two different types of Trill.

a) The Classical Trill which begins on the note above.
b) The Modern Trill which begins on the note itself.

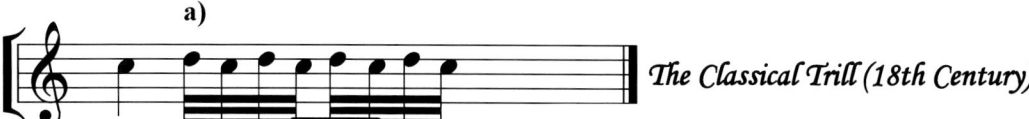

The Classical Trill (18th Century)

The Modern Trill (20th Century)

As we already know 'The Turn' is built from 4 notes, the note above, the note itself, the note below and then the note itself.....

There are three different types of Turn:

The Turn which equals the value of the note.

The Turn which takes half the value of the note before it.

The first 3 notes of the turn equal half the value of the whole note and are written as a triplet, the 4th note of the turn represents the dot which is then joined to the next single note.

The Appoggiatura, the Acciaccatura, and the Inverted Mordent and Turn...

The Appoggiatura

The Appoggiatura always takes half the value of the whole note, the value of the dot is always tied across. b)

The Acciaccatura

The Acciaccatura is a very quick note, normally written as a demisemiquaver. When the ornament appears next to a long note, many ties are required to total the correct rhythm. b)

The Mordent

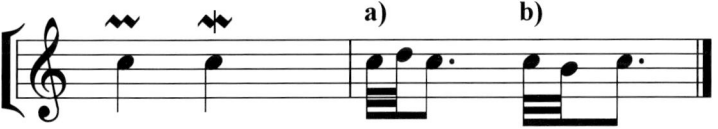

The Mordent can be inverted and is shown with a line through it. The notes written represent the note itself, the note below and then back to the note itself. b)

The Turn

The Turn can also be inverted and like the mordent it is shown with a line through it. The notes written represent the note below, the note itself, the note above and then back to the note itself. b)

…3rd Movement …

The 3rd Movement in a string quartet is normally written in the form of a dance.
(often as a minuet in 3 time)

This movement will be composed using a Ritornello structure.
(A, B, A1)

Task One:

Refer back to the page entitled 'Extending motifs to create a melody'. Three of the motifs are written in 3/4. These tunes will form the basis for this movement. Choose which motif you would like to begin the movement and sketch the notation into one of the instrumental parts.

Task Two:

Create an Um Cha accompaniment between the other three instruments using notes of the triad. (for example: C, E, G in C major)

Task Three:

Through imitation explore different ways of sharing the notes from your three motifs with each instrument. Fill in some of the empty bars with Um Cha accompaniment and different types of ornamentation.
(this will take you to bar 13)

Task Four:

At bar 14 begin a development of the A section. (try experimenting with cross rhythms, different types of ornamentation and introduce a short modulation before bar 29)

Task Five :

Return to the A section at bar 29 but introduce some changes (perhaps some more ornamentation) and finish in the home key.

3rd Movement (a Dance)

Section B (development)

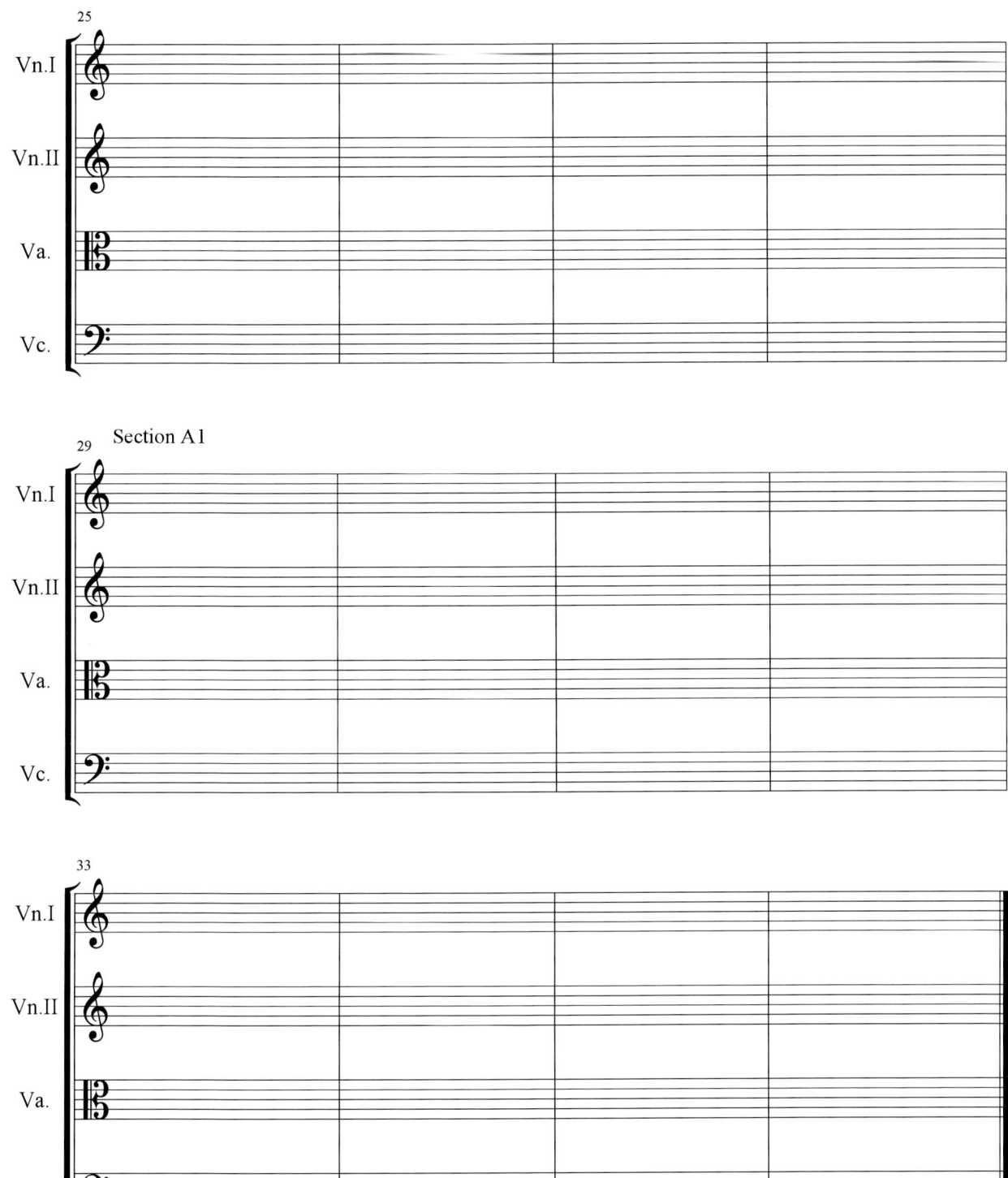

Section A1

...some examples of how to create your 3rd Movement...

Section B (development)

Use of Cross Rhythms

Small Modulation into A Major

Returning to the Home Key

String writing..... some techniques

...4th Movement...

The 4th Movement is often written as a Rondo and each Episode explores
techniques and motivic material used earlier in the string quartet.
Use this movement to experiment with the different playing techniques (arco,
pizzicato, up bows, down bows, string crossing, double stopping etc...)

Task One:

Create a Theme of 4 bars which uses a variety of double stopping, arco and
pizzicato. (you may decide to use material from the main melody, or be creative and
invent something completely different)

Task Two:

Using a variety of resources (material from your main melody, ideas from previous
movements, and all the different playing techniques) create 3 contrasting episodes.
(B, C, and D)

Task Three:

To finish this movement and complete your string quartet, create a Coda which
reflects the material developed in each episode and ties the whole movement
together. It is a good idea if everyone plays together in the last bar, and try and
finish in the home key.

4th Movement (a Rondo)

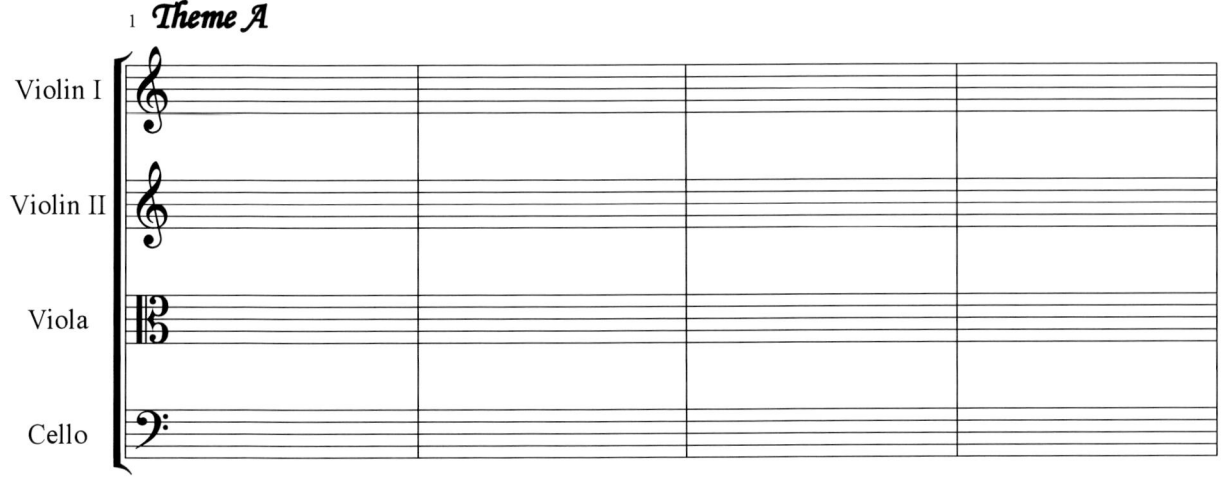

1 **Theme A**

Violin I

Violin II

Viola

Cello

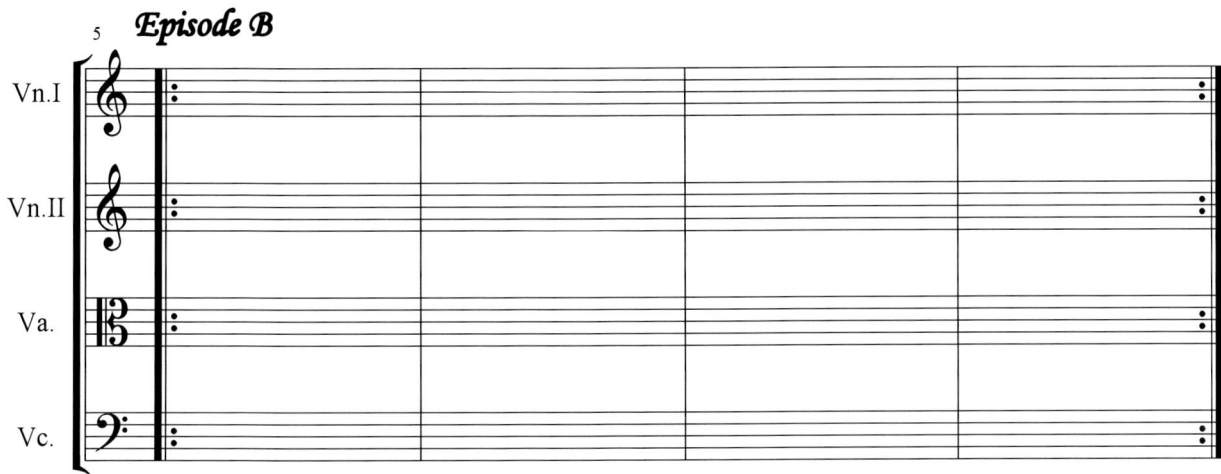

5 **Episode B**

Vn.I

Vn.II

Va.

Vc.

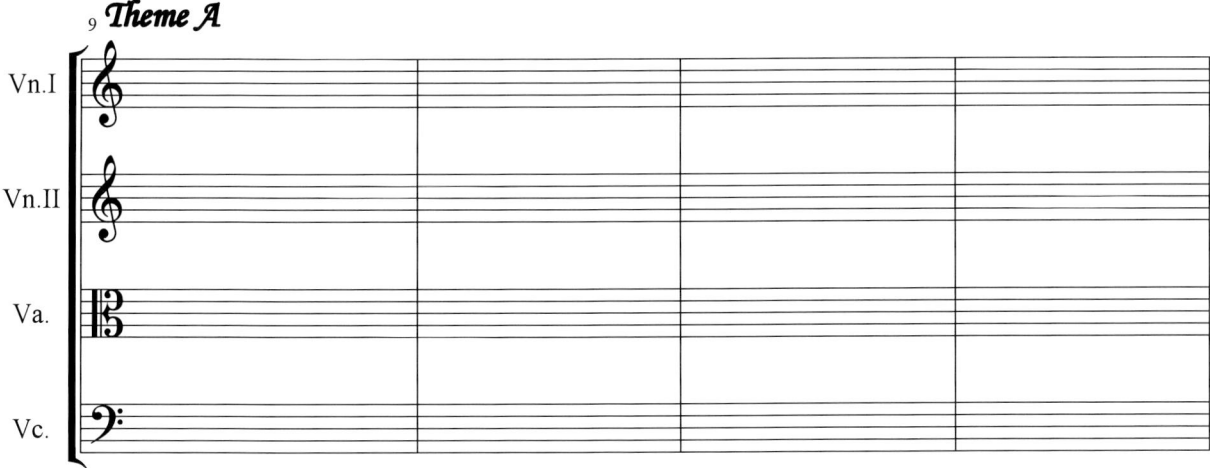

9 **Theme A**

Vn.I

Vn.II

Va.

Vc.

Episode C

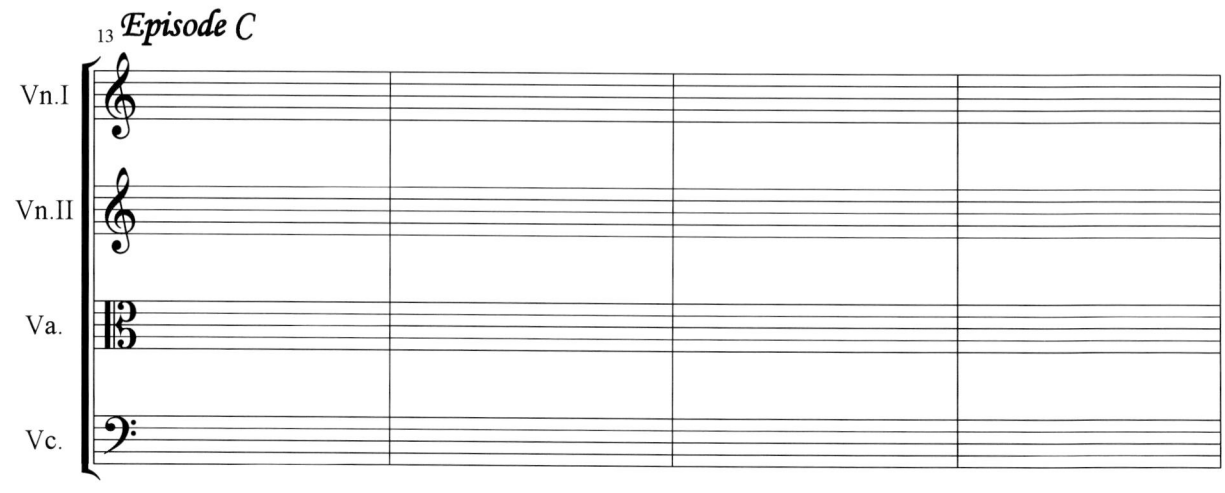

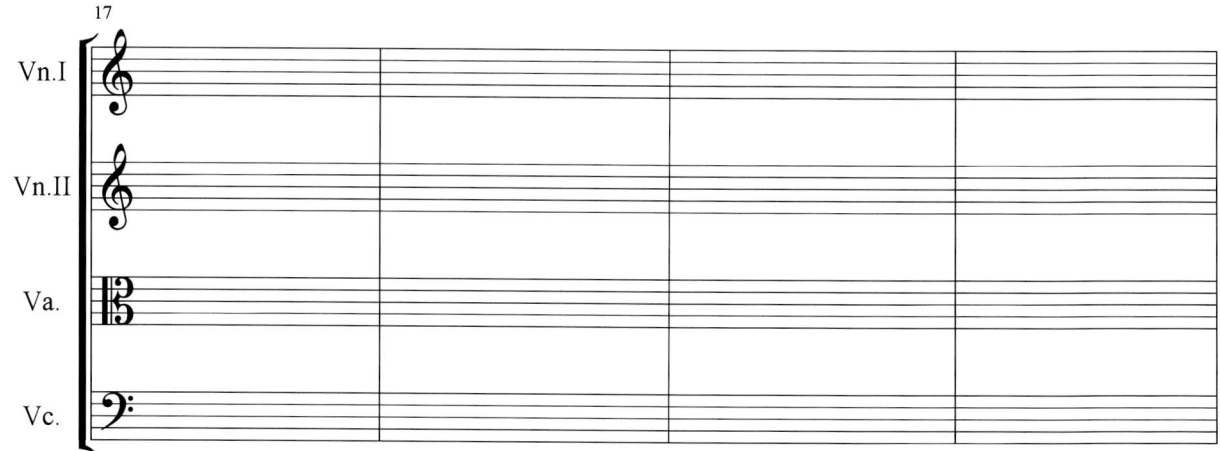

Theme A

Episode D

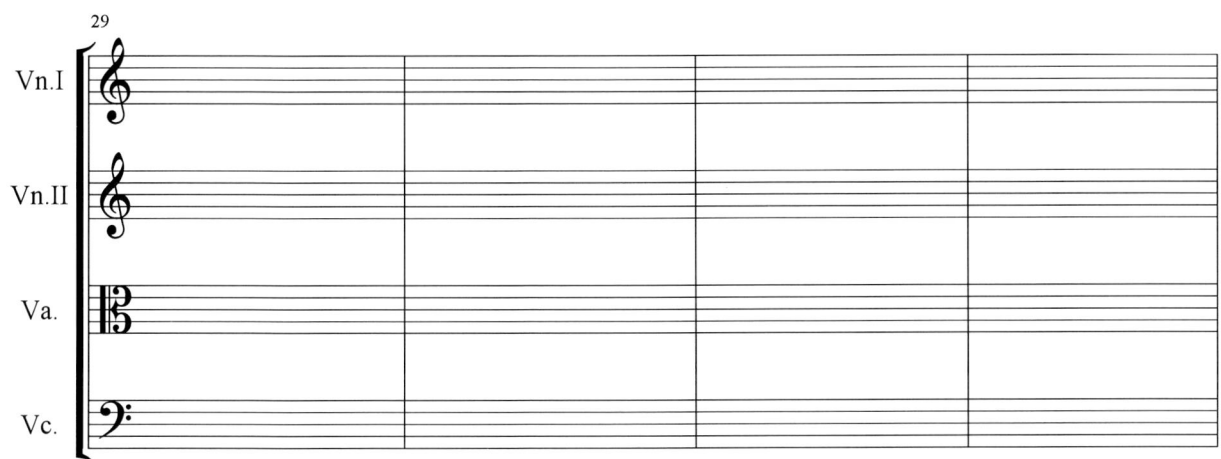

Theme A

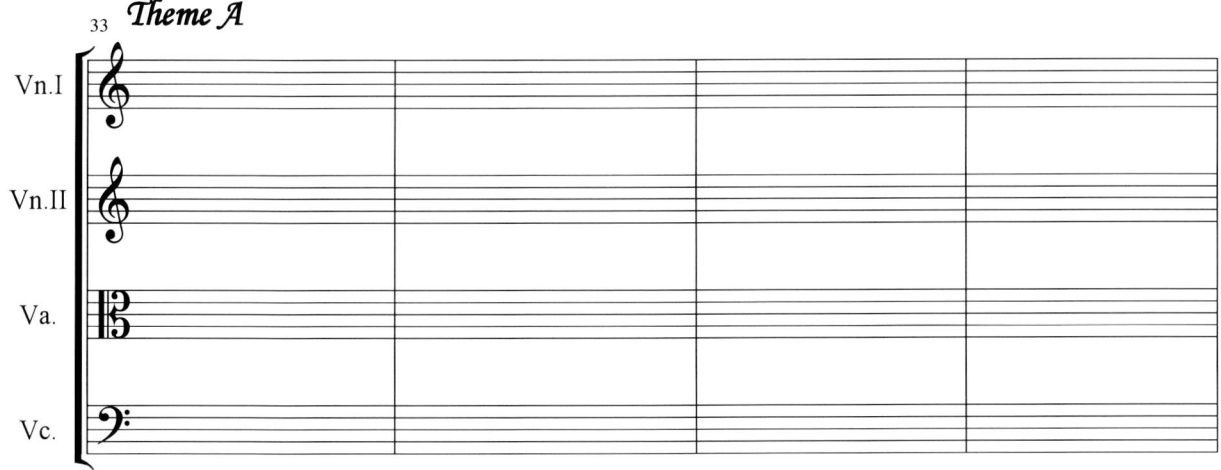

Coda

Examples of how to create your 4th Movement

Episode C

Welcome to the 'Symphony Sizzler.....'

Wolfgang _____ Mozart was only 32 years old when he wrote his symphony number 41. This symphony was given a famous title, today it is better known as the _____ symphony in C major.

To complete this puzzle you need to find the missing parts to the paragraph above using the puzzles on the next three pages to collect clues..... (parts one-seven relate to Mozart's middle name)

When you are collecting clues you will need to convert some of your answers into letters using the alphabet grid on this page. If you put all the letters together they will provide you with the mystery name.......

Good Luck and have fun....!!!

The alphabet grid:

A	B	C	D	E	F	G	H	I	J	K	L	M	N	O	P	Q	R	S	T	U	V	W	X	Y	Z
1	2	3	4	5	6	7	8	9	10	11	12	13	14	15	16	17	18	19	20	21	22	23	24	25	26

Parts One, Two and Three

Part One:

The key of the melody below is _____ spot which note of the scale is absent from the melody. The letter of the missing note is your first clue.

First letter = _____

Part Two:

Calculate the following intervals and then complete the sum below, then convert your answer into a letter using the alphabet grid to find the next clue of the puzzle.

Second letter = _____

_____ ---- _____ ---- _____ = _____

Part Three:

To find the next clue count the number of different rests you can see in the bar below, (for example: 5 crotchet rests, 4 quaver rests etc...) and then complete the paragraph. Once you have done this turn your answer into the next letter using the alphabet grid.

There are _____ quaver rests _____ semiquaver rests and _____ demisemiquaver rests in the bar above. If I add these rests together I would have _____ rests, but of course I have forgotten to count the one beat rests also known as _____ rests of which there are _____ If I divide the total number of one beat rests by the total number of quaver, semiquaver and demisemiquaver rests I would have _____ rests. If I subtract the number of minim rests from my answer _____ I will have the next clue.

Once you have the answer convert the number into the next letter of the puzzle.

Third letter = _____

Part Four:

Which note appears the most in the melody below. The letter name of this note is your next clue in the puzzle. (Use the table below to record the number of times you see each note)

A = _____   C = _____   E = _____   G = _____
B = _____   D = _____   F = _____

Fourth letter = _____

Part Five:

Name the largest interval between two consecutive notes in the melody below. When you have found it, convert it into the next letter using the alphabet grid.   Interval = _____

Fifth letter = _____

Part Six:

Sixth letter = _____

To find the next clue calculate the equation with rests below and then convert your answer into the next letter.

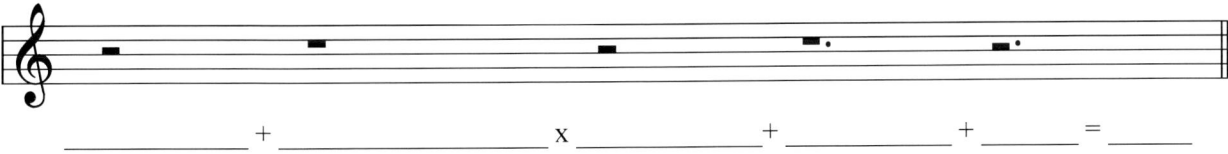

_____ + _____ x _____ + _____ + _____ = _____

Part Seven:

To find the last letter of this part of the puzzle you need to work out how many semiquavers all the notes and rests below equal. Once you have the answer convert it into the last letter.
The answer = _____

Seventh letter = _____

The Last Hurdle...

To find the name of Mozart's Symphony Number 41 try and complete the crossword below.
If you find all the answers using the clues below, you will discover clues which will help
you find 17 down.

Clues going across

1= Type of Brass instrument, has a slide...(8)

4 = Lowest of the woodwind family (7)

7 = Another woodwind instrument (8)

9 = Brass instrument....Don't Beep your...?(4)

11 = Brass instrument..Don't blow your own...? (7)

16 = Common in Jazz and Ragtime (5)

Clues going down

2 = woodwind instrument (nasal sound) (4)

3 = High pitched woodwind instrument (5)

5 = _____Band players....(5)

6 = A Large mixed family of instruments (10)

8= This instrument has strings and pedals (4)

10 = Sounds like a 'mellow' instrument(5)

12 = Lowest of the Brass family (4)

13 = The Viola belongs to the _____ family(6)

14 = Big Bass Drum...? (7)

15 = Lowest of the Orchestral String family (10)

To Find 17 down think of a Planet in the Solar System......

The Name of Mozart's Symphony No 41 = _____

Chapter Four

…Composing a piece for choir…

This chapter will teach you how to compose a complete piece for choir using a variety of skills and tools:

- Exploring the vocal range and singing techniques: melismatic and syllabic.
- Understanding short score and full score.
- Composing techniques which enhance the meaning of the text.

At the end of the chapter, the puzzle 'Voices from around the world' will test your knowledge of composers, important choral works, periods, and compositions from many different countries.

The Vocal Ranges...

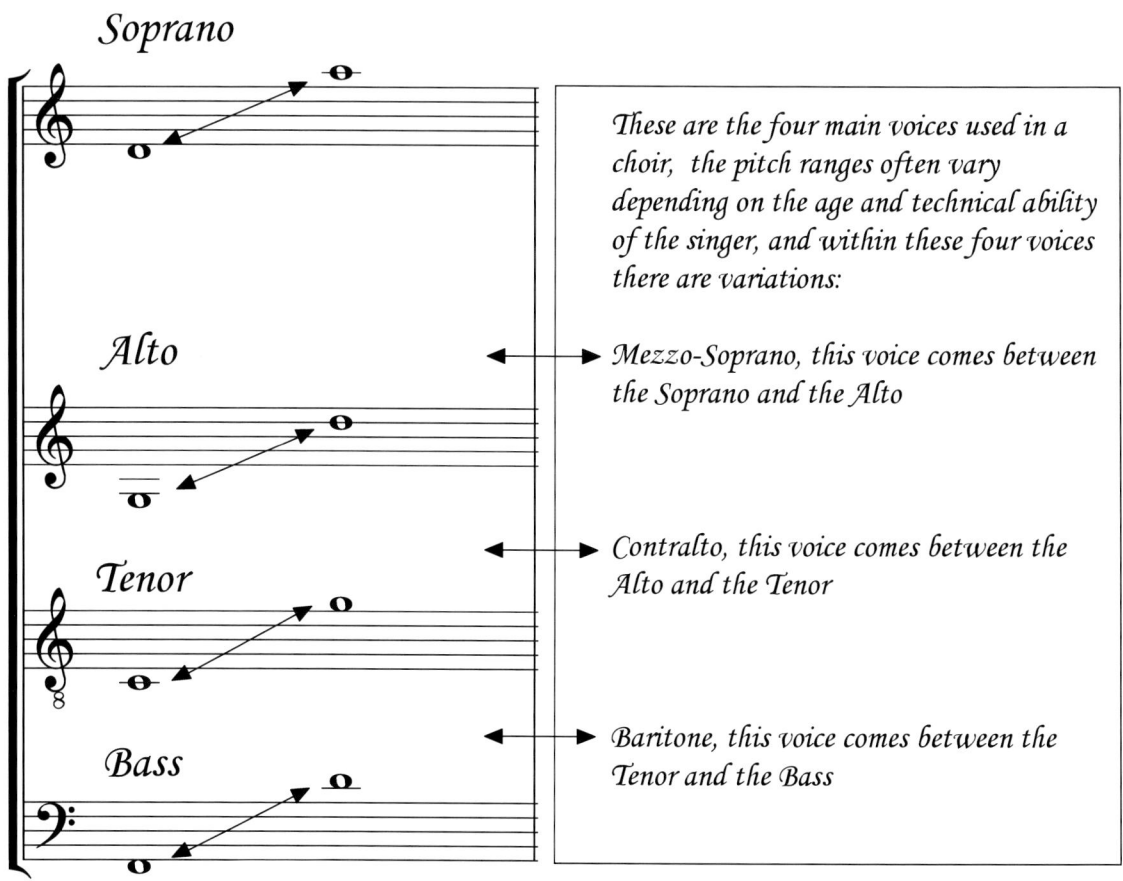

Soprano

Alto

Tenor

Bass

These are the four main voices used in a choir, the pitch ranges often vary depending on the age and technical ability of the singer, and within these four voices there are variations:

Mezzo-Soprano, this voice comes between the Soprano and the Alto

Contralto, this voice comes between the Alto and the Tenor

Baritone, this voice comes between the Tenor and the Bass

There are many ways to compose melodies to words, two of the most common are:

Syllabic, this is when each word or syllable is written under one note.

Melismatic, this is when the words or syllables are stretched over several notes to create melodic decoration.

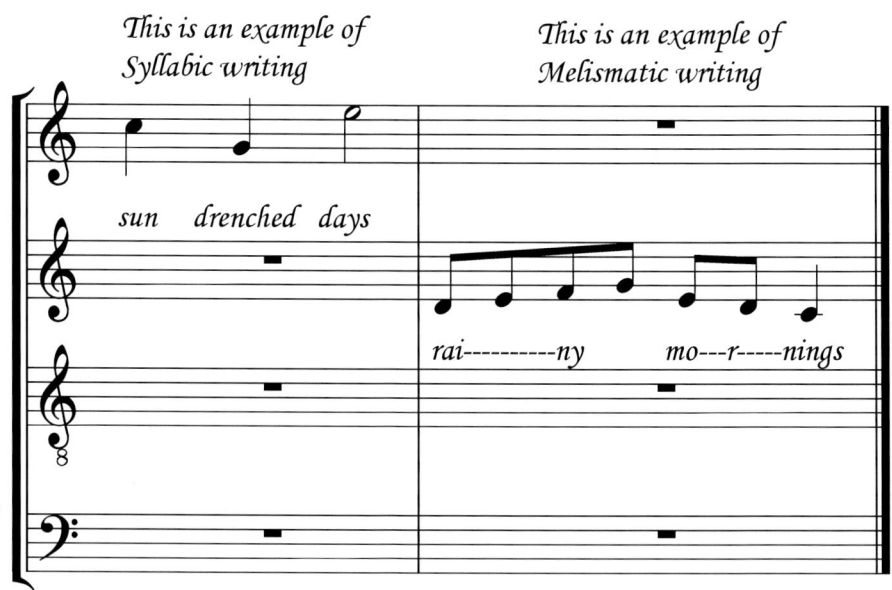

This is an example of Syllabic writing

This is an example of Melismatic writing

sun   drenched   days

rai----------ny   mo---r-----nings

Writing in full score

Task:

Please continue writing in the voices from the short score below.

The piano reduction (also known as the Short score) shows each individual voice by the direction of the note stems.

soprano voice stems are up
alto voice stems are down
tenor voice stems are up
bass voice stems are down

When writing the voices in Full Score the stems go up and down related to the middle line of the stave, but notice how the tenor voice is written in a slightly different treble clef, the 8 underneath tells the performer to sing all these notes an octave lower.

Writing in Short score

(Full Score)

Soprano

alto

tenor

bass

Task:

Please continue writing in the voices from the full score above.

Piano

(Short Score)

Remember:

Soprano voice = note stems up
Alto voice = note stems down
Tenor voice = note stems up
(and an octave lower)
Bass voice = note stems down

The Four Seasons......

Winter:

Down in the valley and over the hill
Whistling winds of a cold winter chill
Bleak from the season and ice that can kill
Darkness is near, and the night is not still

Spring:

Showers are plenty and green is the land
Fast is the river and soft is the sand
Warmth from the sun for the work now in hand
To seed a new life in a world that is grand

Summer:

Days are now longer, months have gone past
Sunsets which fade the evening last, and
Trees with long shadows, of towering mast
Nostalgic emotions of dreams from the past

Autumn:

Strong are the winds that blow the trees dry
Showering leaves in the crimson sky
Crisp in the morning and dark is the night
Winter will come and the land will be white

Written by
Graham Bennett

Writing a melody for soprano voice

> _Task_: Create a melody for soprano voice which uses a variety of techniques in each verse. In addition to rhythmic variations, melismatic and syllabic writing, experiment with different types of melodic movement for example: step, chromatic, leap.

Verse One: _experiment with syllabic writing_

Verse Two: _experiment with melismatic writing_

Verse Three: *explore the use of rests, syncopation and melismatic writing*

Verse Four: *create a strong rhythmic drive using dotted rhythms and syllabic writing*

Examples of writing the tune for soprano voice....

Verse One: _Each syllable is represented by one note..._

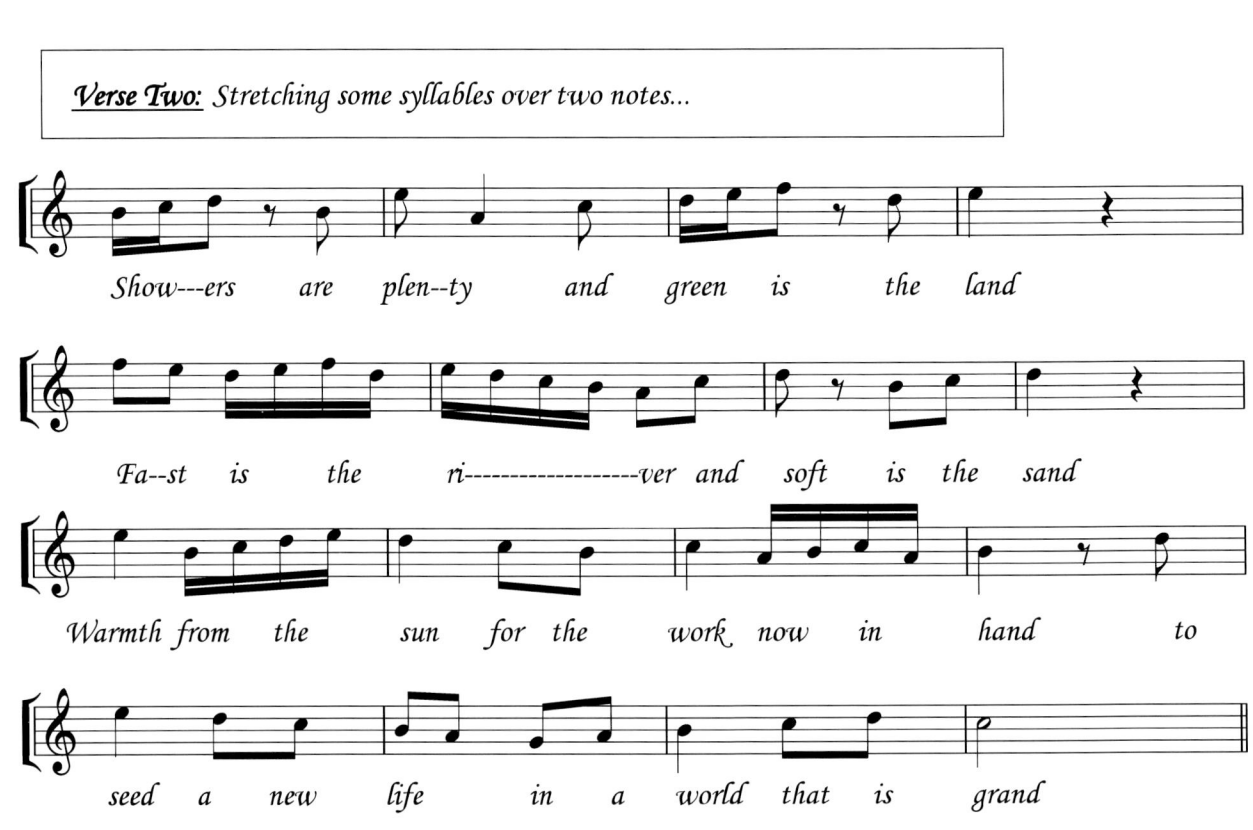

Down in the va-----lley and o--------ver the hill

Whistle-------ing winds of a cold win---ter chill

Bleak from the sea-----son and ice that can kill

Dark---ness is near, and the night is not still

Verse Two: _Stretching some syllables over two notes..._

Show---ers are plen--ty and green is the land

Fa--st is the ri-------------------ver and soft is the sand

Warmth from the sun for the work now in hand to

seed a new life in a world that is grand

Verse Three: *Using rests, stretching the syllables and introducing dotted rhythms...*

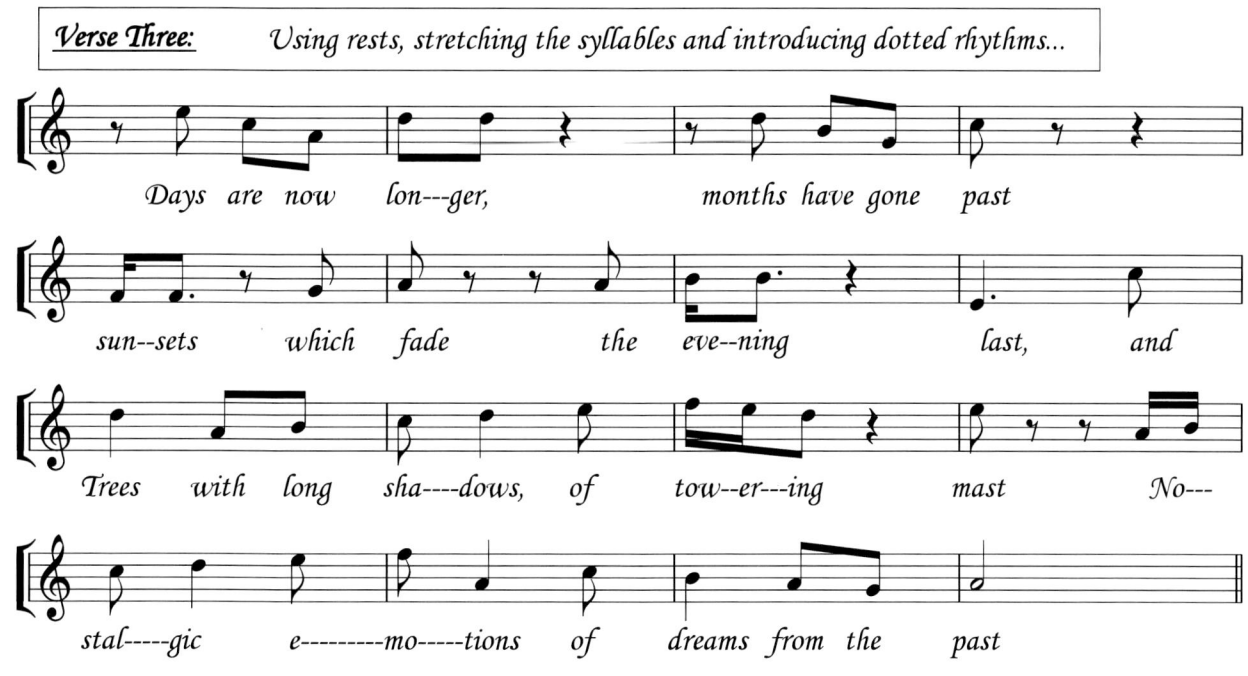

Days are now lon---ger,   months have gone   past

sun--sets   which fade   the   eve--ning   last,   and

Trees   with long sha----dows, of tow--er---ing   mast   No---

stal-----gic   e---------mo-----tions of dreams from the   past

Verse Four: *Creating strong rhythmic drive from dotted rhythms...*

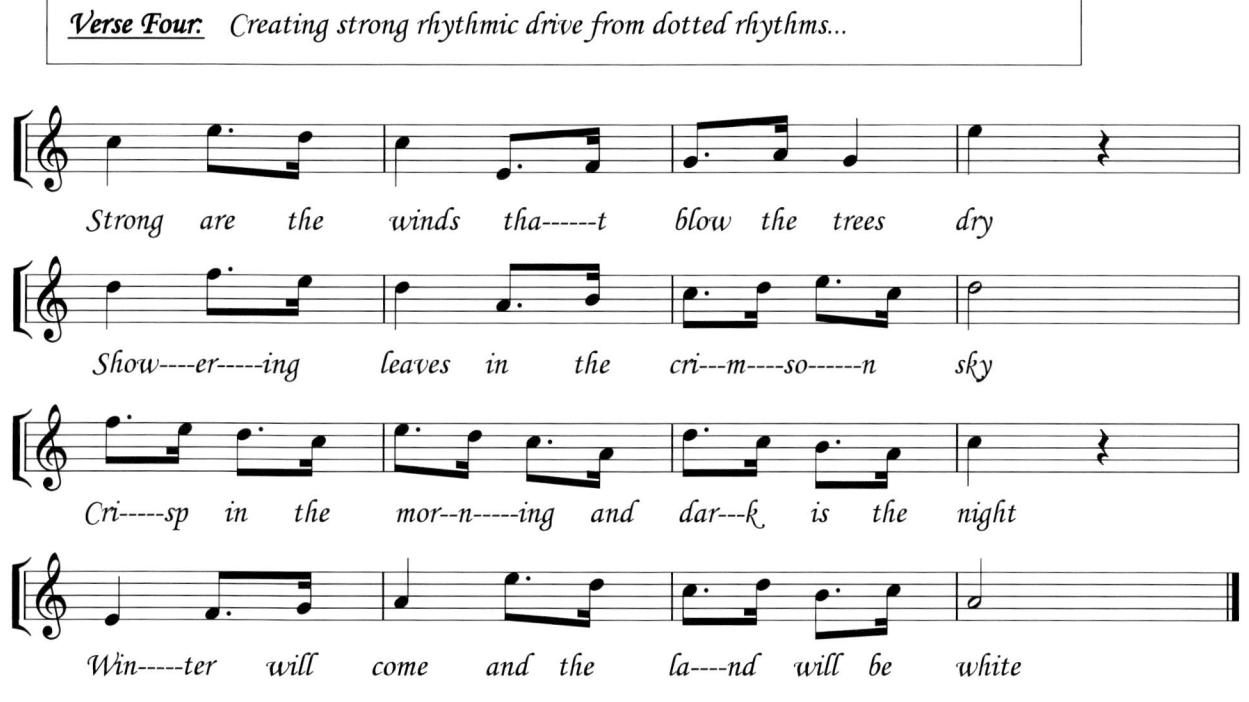

Strong are the   winds tha------t blow the trees   dry

Show----er-----ing   leaves in   the   cri---m----so------n   sky

Cri-----sp in the   mor--n-----ing and dar---k is the   night

Win-----ter will come and the la----nd will be   white

Creating a piece for choir

Task One:

To begin you will need to refer back to your melody for soprano voice. Using the manuscript provided, choose a vocal part (soprano, alto, tenor, or bass) to begin and copy out the first 4 bars of your melody. Each line of the poem will be represented by a different voice, so you will need to transpose the notes accordingly, for example: for line one (4 bars) you may decide to write the melody in the soprano voice, line two (the next 4 bars) you may decide to write the melody in the bass voice which would involve transposing the notes into the bass clef. The vocal entries can be canonic (they can enter in the middle of the previous phrase), or you may choose to bring in each voice at the end of the phrase. (see example (A).

Task Two:

Once you have created your different vocal entries, you can add harmonic colour and reinforce the meaning of the text by filling in some of the other vocal parts. (see example (B). When you are colouring the texture, try using a variety of composing techniques such as melismatic writing, step and leap melodic movement, imitation, ascending and descending phrases to reinforce the importance of certain words. Remember to write the syllables under the notes to indicate how you want each phrase to be sung.

Task Three:

For this task it is important to create a short score in the piano part so that you can check the harmonies between each vocal part (try and avoid dissonances). The short score will also be extremely useful when you begin rehearsals of your piece, the accompanist will be able to work more closely with the singer's intonation if they can see the overall harmonic structure at a glance. (see example (C).

Score layout

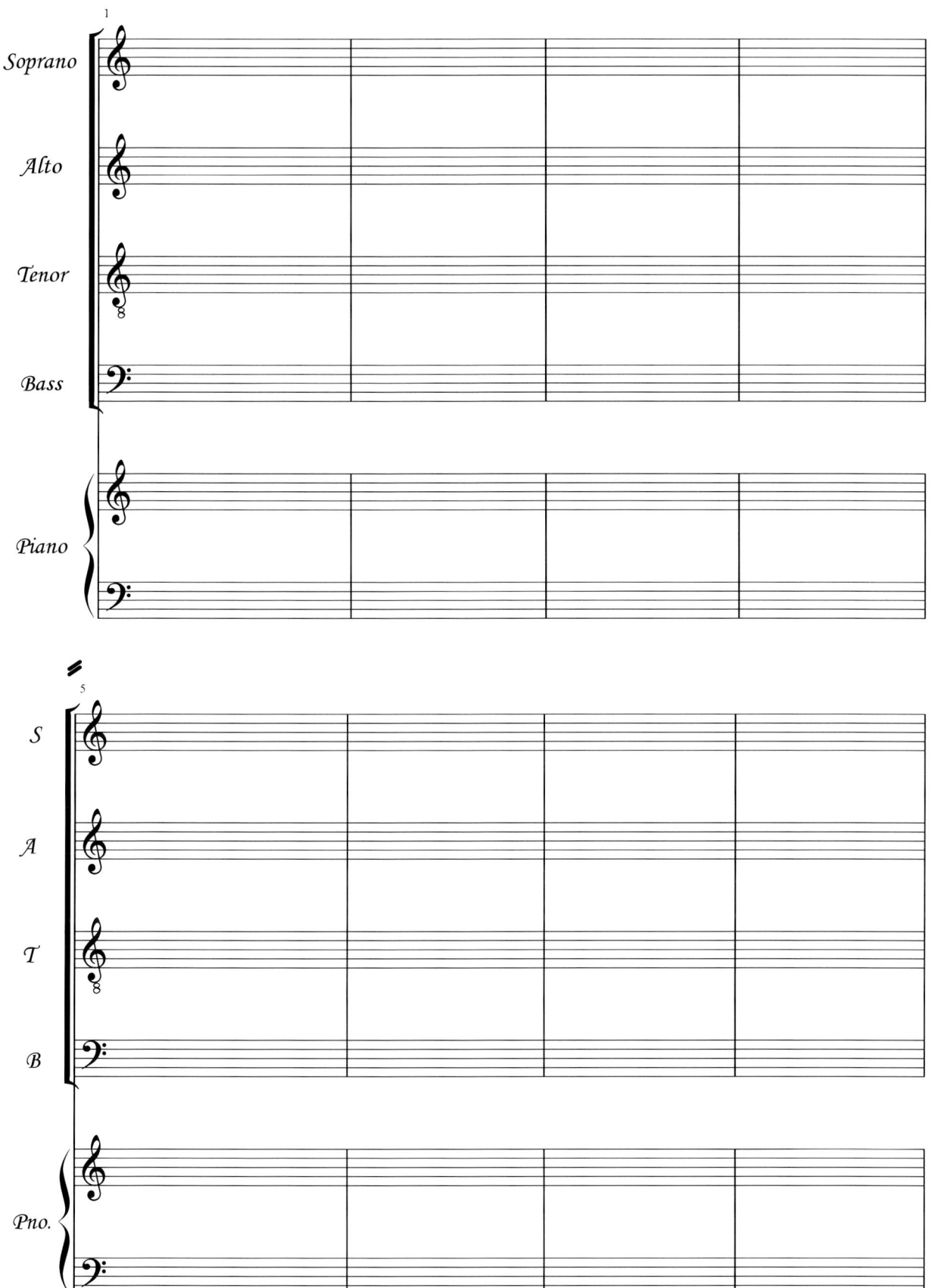

77

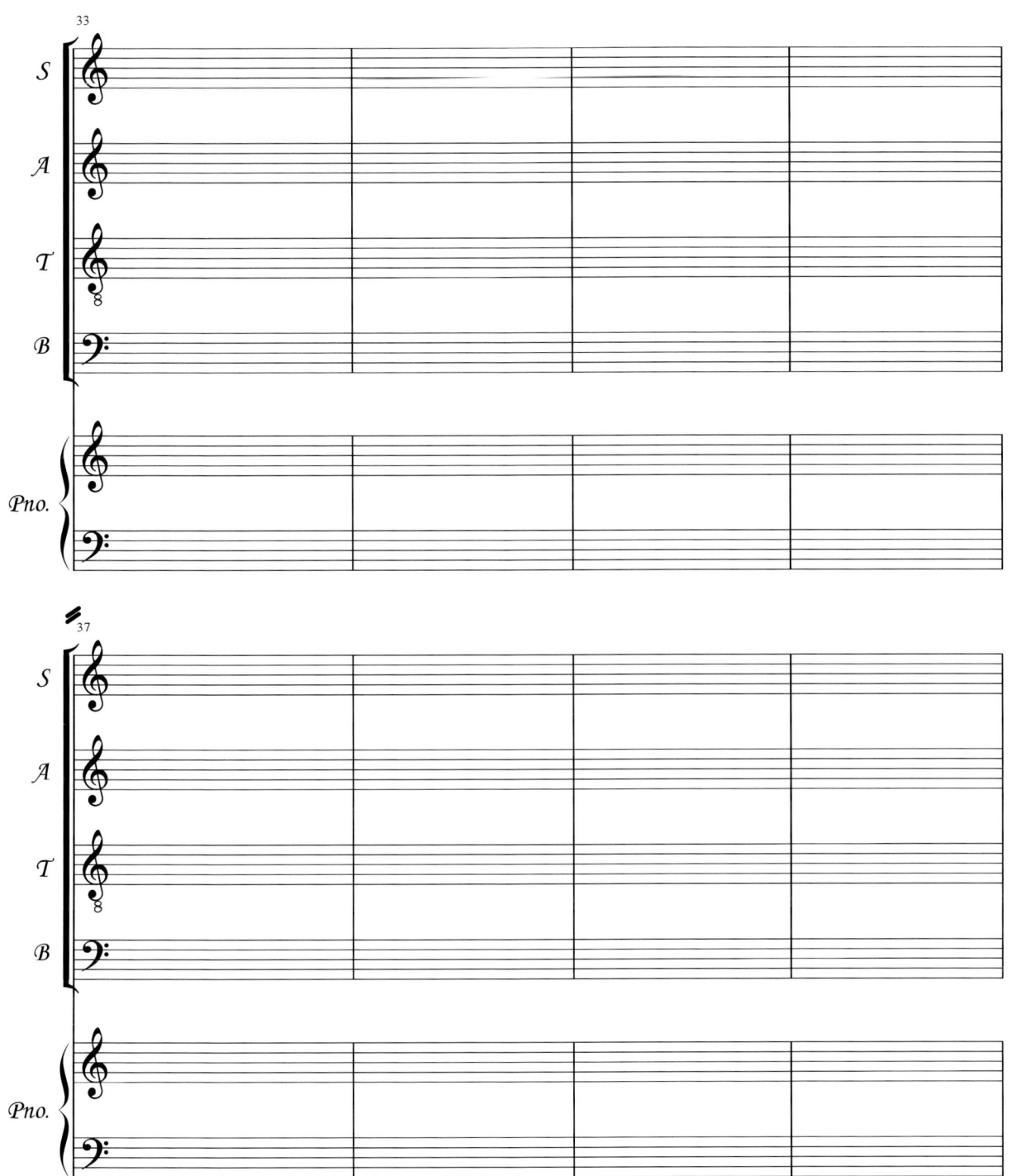

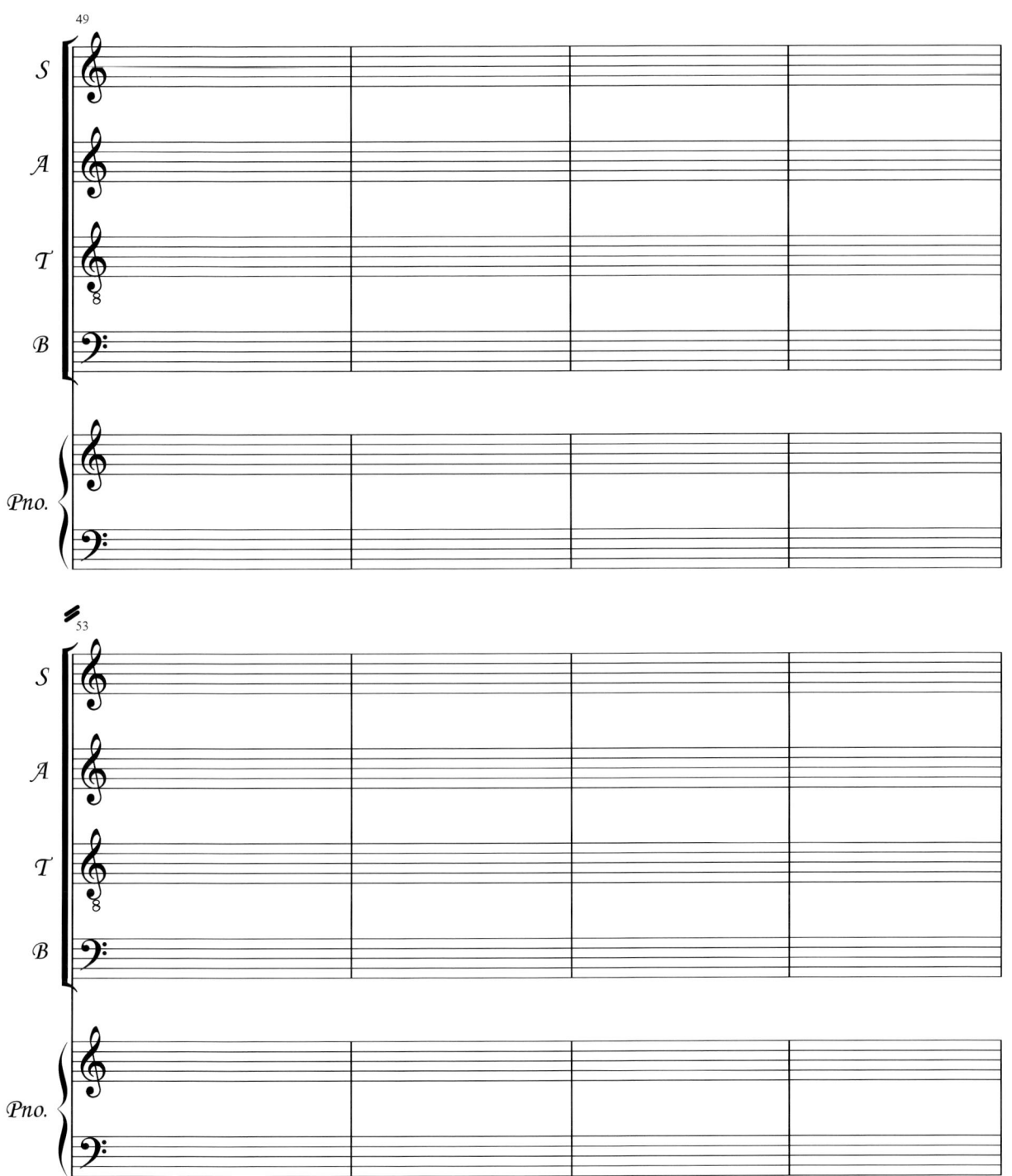

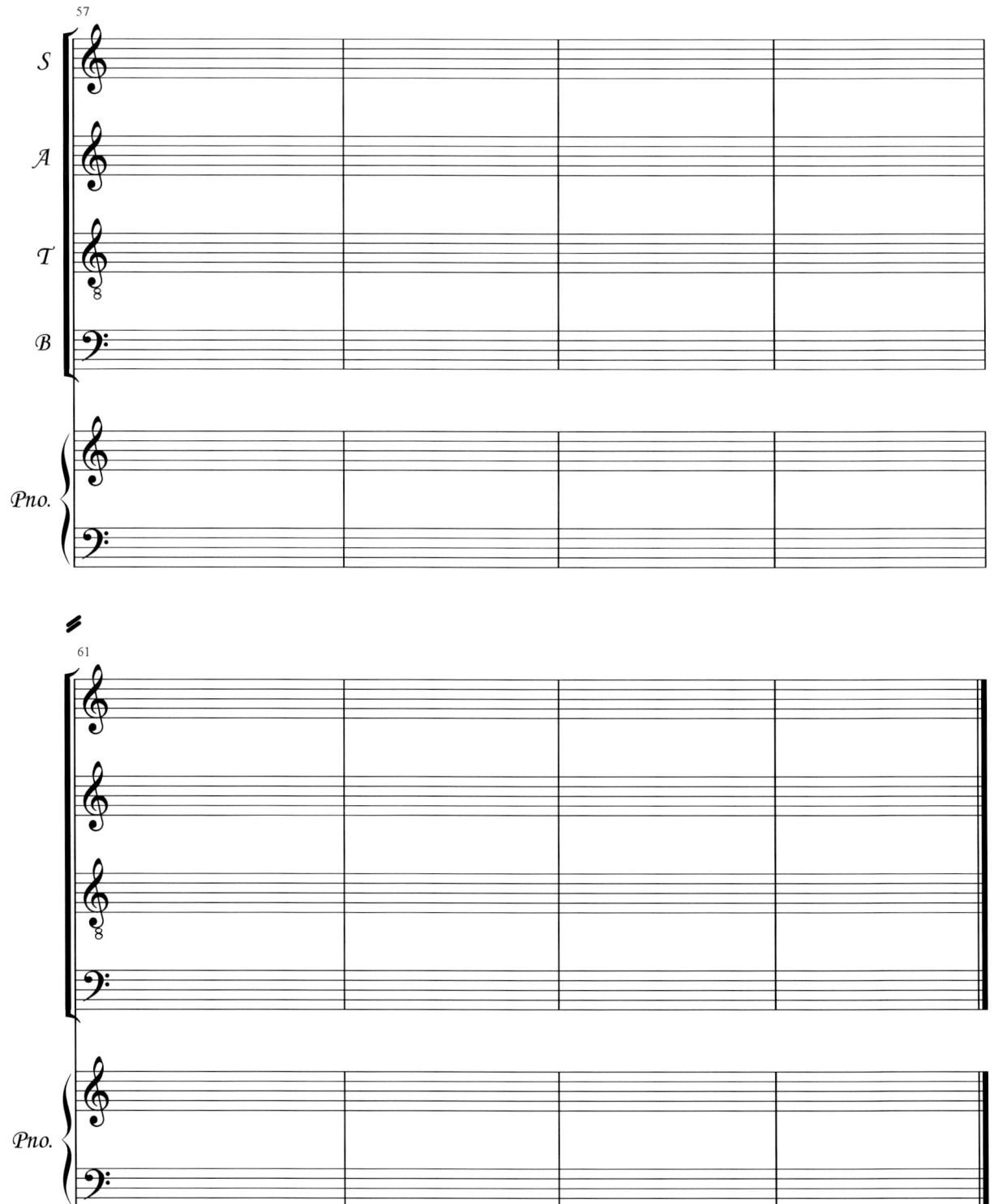

Example (B) (adding colour with the other voices)

Example (C) (creating a short score in the piano part)

Voices from Around the World

To complete this puzzle first you need to follow the trails in the maze……

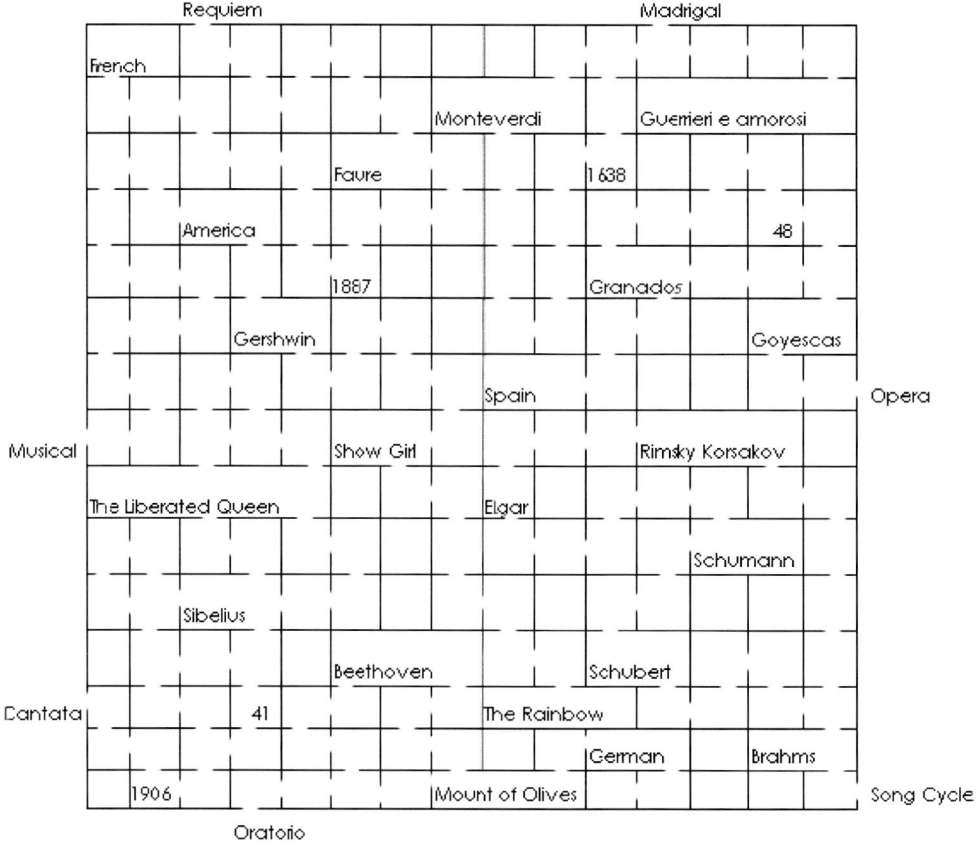

the information in the maze will help you to answer the questions on the next page….have fun and Good Luck

1) Who wrote a Requiem in 1887? _____

1a) What was their nationality? _____

2) Who wrote 'Show Girl'? _____

2a) What type of composition is it? _____

26) Where did they come from? _____

3) How many composers wrote Song Cycles? _____

3a) Who were they? _____

4) What type of composition is 'Mount of Olives'? _____

5) What type of work is 'The Liberated Queen'? _____

5a) Who wrote it? _____

6) What kind of work is 'Goyescas'? _____

6a) Where did the composer come from? _____

7) Can you give the name of another musical? _____

8) Who finished their composition with 48 years old? _____

9) Who was 41 years old in 1906? _____

10) What nationality was Beethoven? _____

11) Who wrote 'Guerrieri e amorosi'? _____

11a) What kind of work is it? _____

116) When was it written? _____

Madrigal

This is a choral work based on secular text; it became popular during the Renaissance period (1450-1600) in Italy and then later in England. The composition is built from many vocal parts woven together using contrapuntal techniques.

Requiem

A Requiem is a Roman Catholic Mass for the Dead, often consisting of many movements, mixed choruses and solos, supported by a full orchestra.

Oratorio

An Oratorio is a large choral work based on text taken from religious topics, for example, 'Messiah' by Handel, and is normally written for soloists, chorus and orchestra.

Musical

A musical always follows a clear plot involving a protagonist and a villain. The stories are often related to love, politics and society. This type of composition uses chorus, soloists, a mix of acoustic and electronic instrumentation, elaborate stage settings and dance.

Cantata

This is a vocal work which can be based on sacred or secular text, and is scored for one or several voices with instrumental accompaniment.

Song Cycle

A song cycle is a group of songs which can be linked together through musical similarities, familiar texts or thematic material, for example, 'Songs of Travel' by Vaughan Williams.

Opera

An Opera represents a drama set to music; the topics can vary considerably from comical to tragedy, love and deceit. This composition incorporates solos known as Arias, with rhythmical speech dialogue known as Recitative, combined with a full orchestra, elaborate stage settings and colourful costumes. It is unusual to have dance in Opera unless it is part of the story.

Chapter Five

...Writing for Jazz Band...

This chapter will teach you how to compose a complete piece for Jazz Band using a variety of techniques and skills including:

- Compositional tools which explore structure, texture and instrumental layering, rhythm, techniques for developing melodic ideas, instrumental breaks, pulse and harmony.
- Working with transposing instruments.
- Writing for drum kit, understanding the notation and techniques.

At the end of the chapter the puzzle 'Name the composer crossword' will test your knowledge of the great masters in Western Classical Music.

Transposing Instruments

Some instruments are naturally transposing instruments which means that the note they read is not the note which is heard when played on their instrument. This means that the composer must re-write their part at a different interval to the other instruments so that the note played is the note the composer wants to hear. For example, the Clarinet in Bb is a transposing instrument. If I ask the clarinettist to play middle C, the note which is heard would be Bb, a major 2nd lower, therefore if I want to hear the note C, I must write the clarinet part a major 2nd higher which would be the note D.

When working out the transposition always relate to middle C.

Trumpet in Bb

Below are the notes written out at Concert Pitch, they represent the notes you will hear when the Trumpeter plays the melody. (ie: a major 2nd lower)

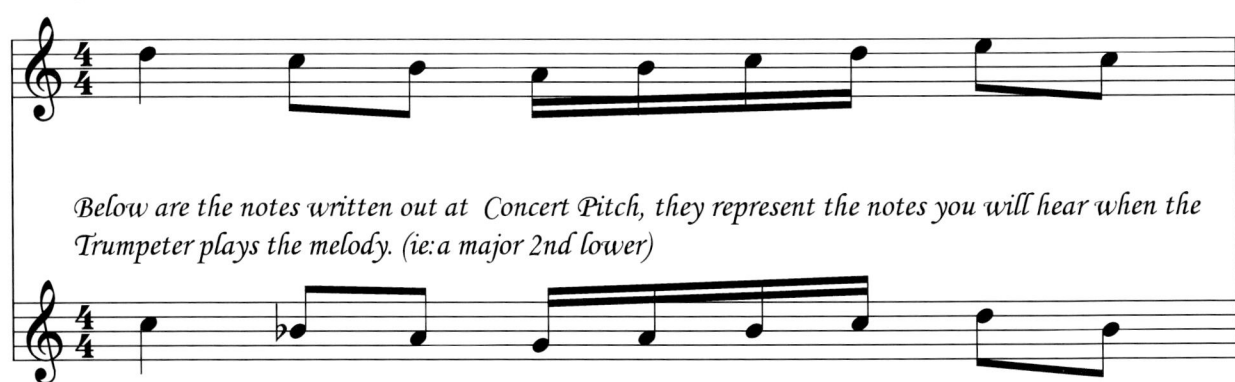

There are many transposing instruments, below are examples of the most common in use today...

The note being played...

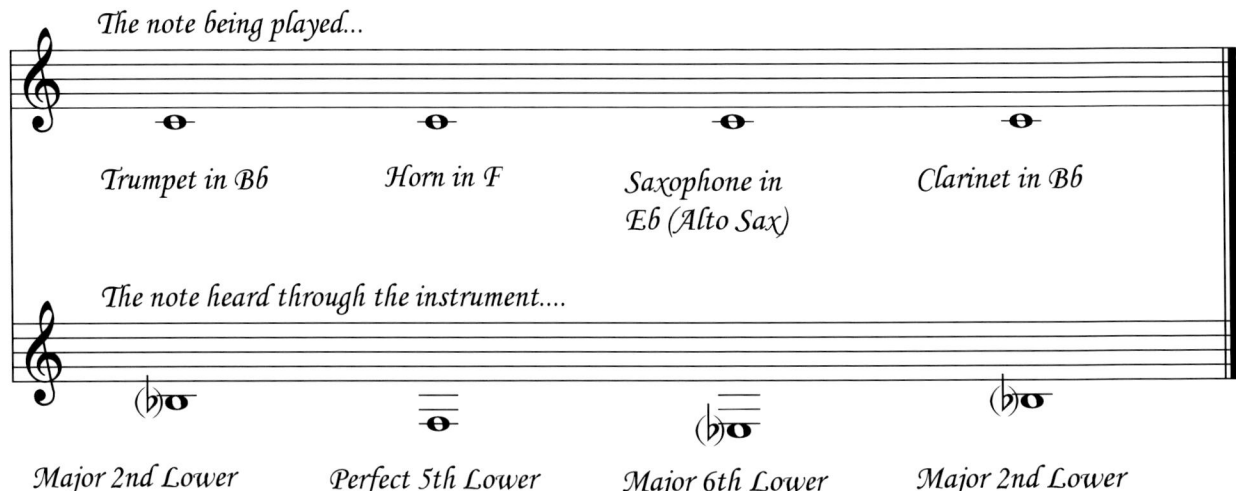

| Trumpet in Bb | Horn in F | Saxophone in Eb (Alto Sax) | Clarinet in Bb |

The note heard through the instrument....

| Major 2nd Lower | Perfect 5th Lower | Major 6th Lower | Major 2nd Lower |

When transposing a melody there are 3 important points to remember....

a) The key signature
(what key is the melody in and what key do you need to transpose into to
represent concert pitch)

b) The intervals when transposing
(if you are transposing down a major 2nd, the interval must be consistent all
the way through the melody)

c) Accidentals
(when you are transposing a melody which contains # or ♭ signs,
remember to adjust the notes at concert pitch so that the intervals remain the same).

Below is a melody written for Eb Saxophone (the Alto Sax)

First look at the melody:

i) it is in the treble clef
ii) the F# in the key signature suggests either G Major or E Minor
iii) The note G appears a lot like a tonic, so we will assume the melody is in G Major.

If we are going to re-write this melody at concert pitch we need to change the key
signature. The Saxophone in Eb transposes down a Major 6th, so the first step is to
create a Major 6th interval between G Major and the new Key.
(remember you need to transpose down)

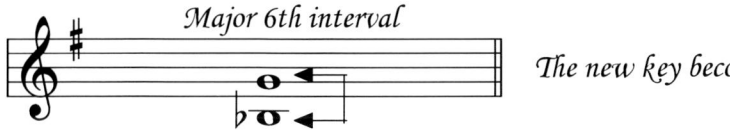

The new key becomes Bb Major

Once I have written in the new key signature, I can transpose all of the notes down a 6th.

Finally, we need to add the accidental. In the original melody the Bb implies that the note has been lowered,
so we must do the same. Bb played at concert pitch would be written as Db. The melody below represents the
finished transposition.

Practice at Transposing Melodies.....

The following melody is written for Clarinet in Bb. Continue writing it out at concert pitch. ie: a major 2nd lower. The Key is E Major, so to create concert pitch I must re-write the melody in D Major.

The following melody is written for Horn in F. Continue writing it out at concert pitch. ie: a perfect 5th lower. The Key is Eb Major, so to create concert pitch I must re-write the melody in Ab Major.

The following melody is written for Trumpet in Bb. Write it out at concert pitch. ie: a major 2nd lower. It is in a major key, remember to add the new key signature.

Writing for Jazz Band....the pitch ranges

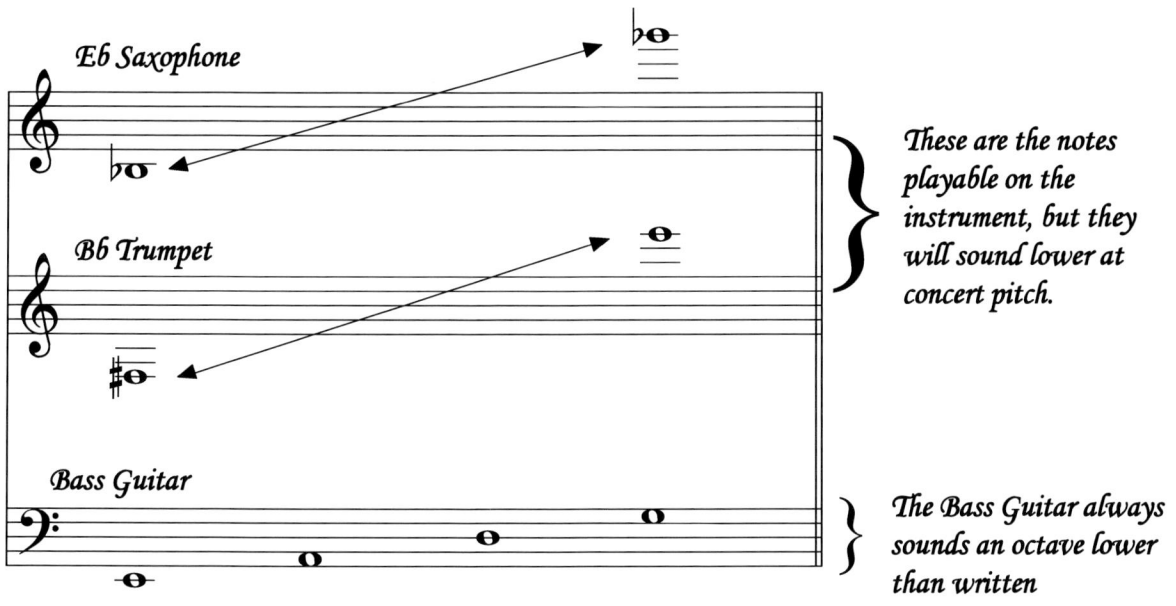

Eb Saxophone

Bb Trumpet

Bass Guitar

These are the notes playable on the instrument, but they will sound lower at concert pitch.

The Bass Guitar always sounds an octave lower than written

A few ideas...

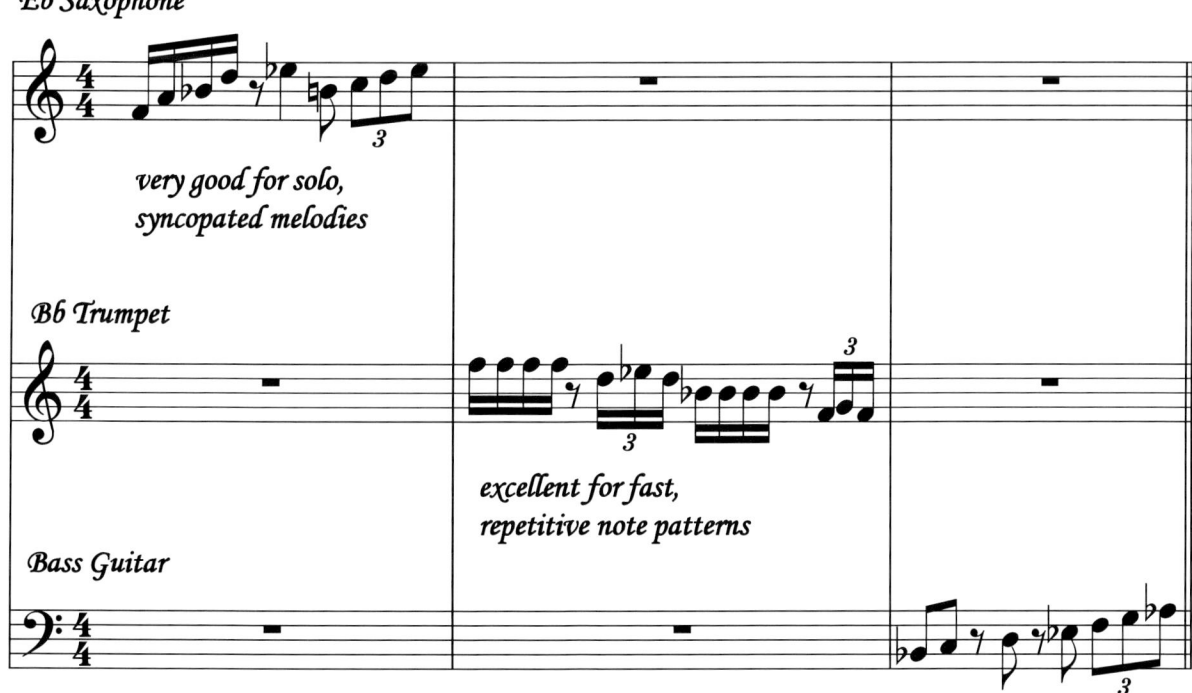

Eb Saxophone

very good for solo, syncopated melodies

Bb Trumpet

excellent for fast, repetitive note patterns

Bass Guitar

famous for creating walking bass lines using dominant 7th harmonies

DRUM KIT NOTATION

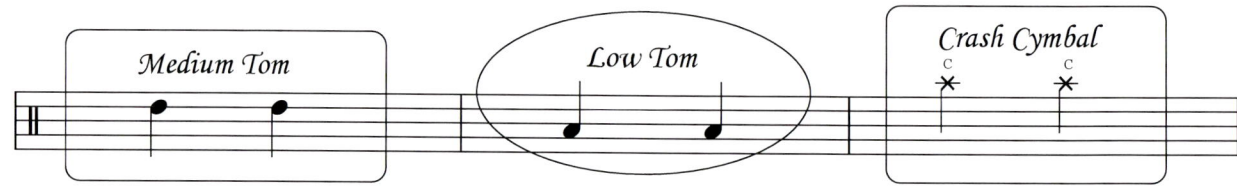

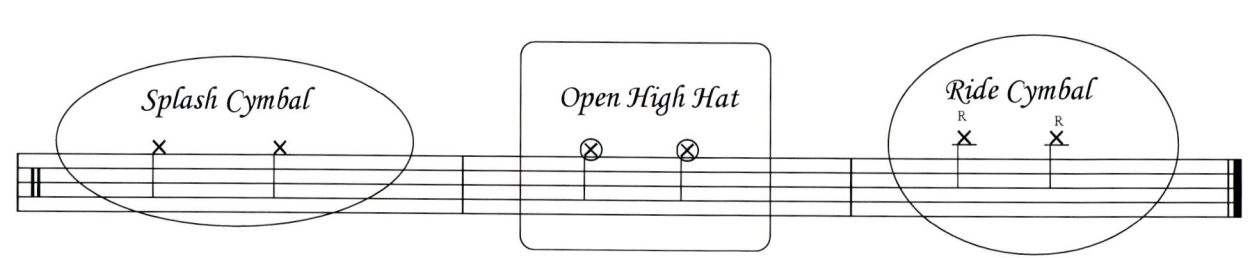

The **Bass Drum** represents the largest drum in the drum kit and is played using a foot pedal which has a large beater attached. This Drum always provides the strongest beat in the rhythm.

The **Tom Tom** drums vary in size. They are played with wooden drum sticks, the smallest creates a shallow sounding beat, the largest creates a deeper sounding beat.

The **Cymbals** vary, the splash and ride cymbals create an explosion of sound (similar to shattered glass...very effective at a climax in the piece)

The **Open High Hat** consists of two cymbals which clash together with the use of a foot pedal. These cymbals are very effective on the off-beats.

The **Snare Drum** can be played with a wire brush or with wooden sticks, the metal springs underneath the drum create an effective rattle which can be used to reinforce different beats in the rhythm.

Let's write a piece for Jazz Band…

Before you write a piece for Jazz Band, it is important to think about the following ingredients:

Structure

for this composition let's use exposition, development and recapitulation with a coda at the end

Texture and instrumental layering

bring the instruments in gradually

Rhythm

use a variety of different rhythmic techniques…cross rhythms, syncopation etc…

Techniques for developing melodic ideas

repetition, sequence, imitation, contrary motion, step and leap movement

Instrumental breaks

solo instrumental sections, tutti (where everyone plays together)

Pulse

where do you want the strong beat to come…on beats 1 and 3, or 2 and 4…

Harmony

try and use a mixture of diatonic triads, notes within the key and 7th chords. Perhaps experiment with chromatic harmonies including Augmented 6th chords, and modulation

Examples of writing for Jazz Band

Notice the different key for the Saxophone and Trumpet parts. These parts have been transposed .

add drum beats (bass drum for strong beats, ride cymbal for soft beats) and create contrasting rhythms where the instrumental texture is thin.

solo (exposure)

Coda

more rhythmic variation

descending phrases
(contrast with exposition)

Writing the Exposition:

Task One:

Decide on a key signature for the Exposition and write in the sharps or flats at the beginning of each instrumental part.

Task Two:

Create a walking Bass melody of two bars using a mixture of ascending and descending notes in step movement.

Task Three:

At bar 3 introduce the piano part using simple triads or 7th chords to support the walking bass melody.

Task Four:

At bar 5 bring in the drums. Decide which beats are going to be the strongest (1 and 3, or 2 and 4). Use Bass drum for the strong beats and the ride cymbal or open high hat for the weaker beats. In bar 6 create a contrasting rhythm by mixing in other drum beats. Show the different beats by writing note stems up and down. (see examples)

Task Five:

At bar 9 introduce the Trumpet. (transpose the notes a major 2nd higher) Create a melody which contrasts the Bass Guitar part and demonstrates more rhythmic variety.

Task Six:

At bar 13 bring in the Saxophone. (transpose the notes a major 6th higher) This melody should be more independent rhythmically and melodically. (use a variety of step, leap and chromatic notes, and experiment with syncopation).

Task Seven:

Continue/develop each instrumental part up to bar 20. You may decide to introduce a solo, or vary the saxophone and trumpet parts, or change the drum beat, or perhaps introduce more variety in the piano part. Keep the development simple, too much change at once can effect the momentum and character of your piece. Repetition is an important ingredient in Jazz.

Writing the Development Section

Once you have completed tasks one to seven and you are happy with the Exposition, you can create a development section by using some of the tools mentioned below:

a) Modulate to the relative minor and experiment with sequential writing to move back and forth through the two keys. You can also explore other keys using a variety of accidentals in different instrumental parts. In the example, the development section begins at bar 21 in G minor (the relative minor of Bb major) but there is always a feeling that the section is still in the home key.

b) Create more rhythmic variation and imitation between the instrumental parts. In the example, the Bass Guitar plays a triplet pattern in bar 23, this rhythm creates a link into bar 24 where the rhythm is then taken over in the drums. In bar 27 there is an example of rhythmic imitation between the trumpet and piano.

c) Instrumental solos and exposure of rhythmic and motivic patterns. In the example, the Saxophone plays an exposed melodic and syncopated fragment (taken from bar 25 in the exposition) accompanied only by the piano semiquaver chords and at the end of the development section the drums play a solo from bar 38 to bar 40.

Writing the Coda Section

The coda is the final section of the composition and should contain some material used previously, combined with some additional developments in texture, rhythm and tonality. In the example, the Bass Guitar begins with the descending melodic idea first used in bar 2 of the exposition, but in the coda it becomes an ostinato up to bar 67. The Trumpet and Saxophone provide a rhythmical dialogue of triplets, quavers and dotted notes from bar 61 to bar 63. The piano enters at bar 64 using harmonies which suggest both Bb major and G minor. The drum part is very simple using only the crash cymbal to keep the pulse, but there is a build up of tension towards the end in bar 67 using triplets and more of the drum kit. As the piece moves closer to the final bar, all the instruments come in to form a tutti in the home key.

The Jazz Band Score

Exposition

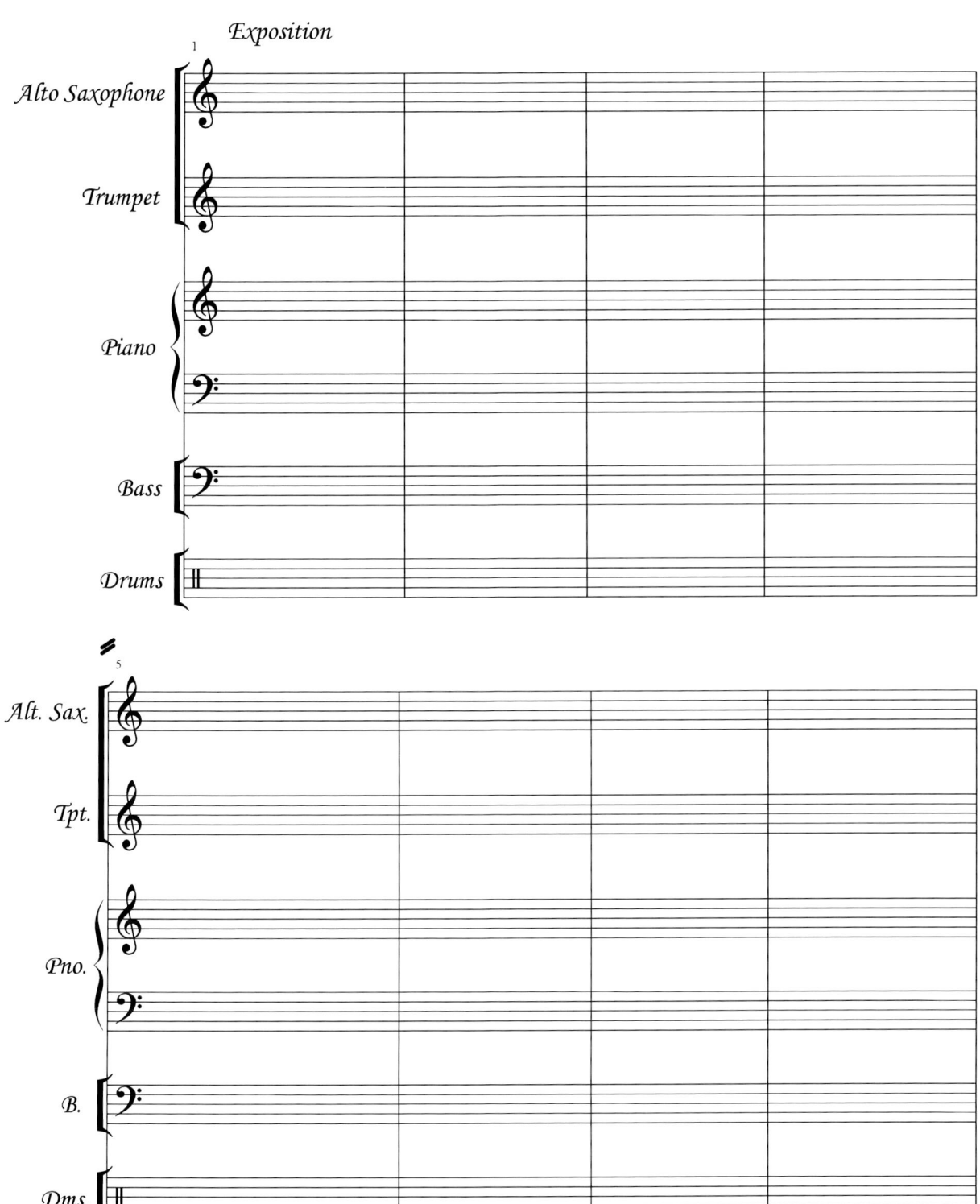

Development

Recapitulation

Coda

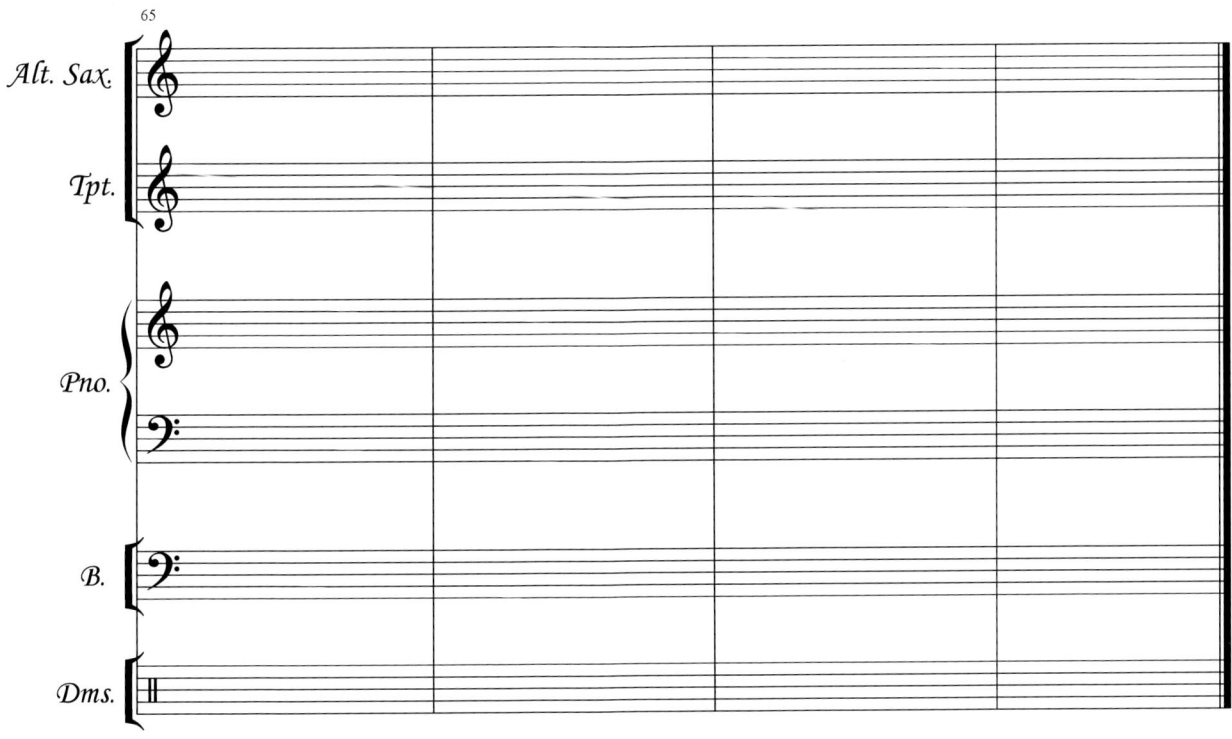

Name the composer crossword

To complete this crossword use the clues below......Have fun !!!!

The composers...

Haydn

Brahms

Liszt

Mahler

Dukas

Balakirev

Schubert

Kodaly

Borodin

Mozart

Cage

Holst

Elgar

Berlioz

Tchaikovsky

Sibelius

Clues across

1 = Finlandia (a symphonic poem)

2 = 'Surprise' Symphony

3 = Opera 'Beatrice et Benedict'

5 = 1812 Overture

7 = Enigma Variations

10 = Sorcerer's Apprentice

11 = Fantasia on Hungarian folk themes

13 = Symphony No2 'Resurrection'

Clues down

4 = Ballet 'Spartacus' (also founded school of singing)

6 = 'The Planets'

8 = Opera 'Don Giovanni' (also wrote the magic flute)

9 = '4 minutes 33 seconds' (compound with metal bars)

12 = German Reqium

14 = Opera 'Prince Igor'

15 = 'Trout' Quintet

16 = 'Islami' a piano fantasy (also one of the 'mighty handful